People's Democratic Platform, 2004

★ ★ ★ ★ ★

People's Democratic Platform, 2004

★ ★ ★ ★ ★

For the Restoration of a Democratic Republic

THE TERRA NOVA SERIES
North Atlantic Books
Berkeley • California

Published by
North Atlantic Books
P.O. Box 12327
Berkeley, California 94712

Cover and book design by Paula Morrison
Printed in the United States of America
Distributed to the book trade by Publishers Group West

People's Democratic Platform, 2004 is sponsored by the Society for the Study of Native Arts and Sciences, a nonprofit educational corporation whose goals are to develop an educational and crosscultural perspective linking various scientific, social, and artistic fields; to nurture a holistic view of arts, sciences, humanities, and healing; and to publish and distribute literature on the relationship of mind, body, and nature.

Library of Congress Cataloging-in-Publication Data

The people's democratic platform.
p. cm. — (The terra nova series)
ISBN 1-55643-498-7 (pbk.)
1. Democratic Party (U.S.)—Platforms. 2. Presidents—United States—Election—2004. 3. Populism—United States. 4. Political planning—United States. 5. United States—Politics and government—2001– I. Society for the Study of Native Arts and Sciences. II. Series.
JK2316.P46 2004
324.2736—dc22

2004008805

1 2 3 4 5 6 7 8 9 DATA 09 08 07 06 05 04

Contents

★ ★ ★ ★ ★

The *People's Democratic Platform* is a collaborative effort of dozens of people, some of whom contributed many pages, others a mere comment or quote. Some contributors wrote on many topics, most on just one. We have elected not to name all the contributors, as the individual contributions have been rewritten and subsumed in the single voice of the document itself. The document was synthesized out of its many pieces by Alan S. Kay, with editorial assistance from staff at Terra Nova/North Atlantic Books.

The goal of this project was not to assemble a patchwork anthology of opinions and ideas or cover every issue, but to offer for consideration a sense of the collective voice—to borrow a phrase from the primary campaign—of the Democratic wing of the Democratic Party. Since the party's candidate selection is now a done deal, what debate there may be will focus on the positions that the candidate should espouse. We seek to influence that debate, to remind the party of its roots and tradition, and to provide a counterbalance to the inevitable tendency to move to the right to seize ground from the Republicans. That would be a mistake.

Many of the people who will vote for the Democratic presidential candidate this fall will disagree on numerous points in this document. Our 2004 "People's Platform" is more radical than the one the Democratic Party will adopt, but it is still Democratic. The editors kept within the mainstream of Democratic politics even where their own politics called for more liberal statements.

In a nation acutely polarized between "red" and "blue" factions, as they are commonly represented on an electoral map of the states, we want to capture the collective blue yelp of the Democratic donkey—angry, hopeful, betrayed, idealistic, still believing in the compassionate and progressive side of humanity.

PREAMBLE

★ ★ ★ ★ ★

Four score and a hundred forty-seven years ago, our fathers and mothers brought forth upon this continent a new nation, conceived in liberty, and dedicated to the proposition that all men and women are created equal.

We are the Americans who still believe in the universal application of that proposition.

Because of this, we are engaged in a great civil war. There is no other way to put it. Against us are ranged the powerful and well-financed partisans of a plutocratic national security state—a state founded immediately after World War II; a parasite state erected on top of the democratic republic constituted by Franklin and Washington; a deluded state which in its quest to prevent every possible fantasy attack, has neglected to define the nature and origin of the real threats that face us.

Under the name of national security, this parasite state has the power to suspend the rule of law—to search without warrant, to imprison without due process.

Under the name of national security, it has the power to label its actions "top secret," and to shield them from any public scrutiny, not simply while these actions are being undertaken, but for years afterwards.

Under the name of national security, it has the power to designate enemies without any kind of public discussion, and to initiate warlike actions against them.

Under the name of national security, it has established military bases in seventy-five foreign countries staffed by troops who are inevitably perceived as alien overlords by the populations through which obliviously they stride.

Under the name of national security, it permits itself to tax and spend to rebuild schools and infrastructure abroad while denying public funds for domestic needs.

What long series of abuses has brought us to this pass? How did we go to bed with the Bill of Rights and wake up with the Patriot Act? How did we suffer the results of a coup without undergoing the actual coup itself? How did we acquire an empire without ever having voted for one? When will we recover a decent respect for the opinions of mankind?

About these matters there can be disagreement, but at least one truth is still self-evident: a house divided against itself cannot stand.

Neither America, nor any other country, can live half-democratic and half-dictatorial. It will become all one thing or all another.

No democracy can survive with leaders whose campaign goals dictate keeping the American people in a constant state of fear and anxiety.

No democracy can survive a state of permanent national emergency.

No democracy can survive by manufacturing endless enemies.

No democracy can survive without transparency of information and accountability of public officials.

We believe in a limited notion of defense: the protection of the continental United States and the protection of its citizens.

We do not acknowledge any vague "vital interests" to be protected beyond these.

We do not acknowledge vague and unending "world responsibilities."

We do not acknowledge a uniquely American right to act as we see fit, subject to no law other than our will—a "right" accorded to no other country.

Our choice is not only between empire and collective security.

It is between an empire and a democratic republic—the one whose birth we justly celebrate every Fourth of July.

We do not expect these United States to be dissolved; we do not expect this house to fall; but we do expect it to cease to be divided.

It will become all one thing or all the other.

Either the opponents of the dictatorial national security

state shall arrest the further spread of it and place it where the public mind shall rest in the belief that it is in the course of ultimate extinction, or its advocates shall push it forward till it shall replace the one the framers founded.

In the hope of rallying all Americans to dismantle this parasite state, in the belief that only by doing so can the mechanisms of democracy operate again, we offer this platform.

I. PEACE AND JUSTICE

Not since the Vietnam war has the population of the United States been so divided as it is today by the decision of our government to expend massive quantities of our resources and expose to harm the men and women of our armed forces. Far from uniting the country, President Bush has polarized the United States at a time when our role in world affairs will be a critical determinant of the shape of the world and the condition of its many inhabitants for the foreseeable future.

The image of Iraq that sprang to most Americans' minds when they learned that the Bush administration had begun rattling sabers in its direction—an image of little beige tents set up on the sides of dirt roads, men and boys riding about on their camels, donkeys, and goats while girls and women sit at home, wearing black burkas, making bread and taking care of lots of little children—is a myth.

In fact, as the Girl Blogger of Baghdad has pointed out in her Internet commentary, Iraqis are people just like us. They live in houses with running water and electricity. Thousands of them own computers. Millions own VCRs and CD players. Iraq has bridges, recreational centers, clubs, restaurants, shops, universities, and schools. Iraqis love fast cars, and the Tigris is full of motorboats that are used for everything from fishing to water-skiing.

There is no question that Saddam Hussein was a brutal dictator. But we reject the claim that that fact alone was sufficient to justify the unilateral U.S. armed intervention in Iraq that has wreaked havoc with the lives of the Iraqi people. And we reject even more strongly the attitude toward representative government reflected in the lies concerning alleged weapons of mass destruction offered to justify the armed incursion. That Democratic members of Congress allied themselves with this sham does nothing to excuse this adventuristic campaign.

We reject the view of the United States as the world's policeman. As the Democratic Party wrote in its 2000 Platform, "In the wake of the Cold War, America has entered a new Global Age that is altering our security challenges and creating entirely new issues. Globalization is transforming the international order that defined the 20th century. Today, for both good and ill, our destiny and the destinies of billions of people around the world are increasingly intertwined. . . ."

We believe our flag ought to stand for principles of freedom, equality, and democracy. But much of the rest of the world is predisposed to view the United States as a self-aggrandizing bully. We are, after all, the country that possesses the lion's share of the world's weapons of mass destruction. Unilateral military incursions, however well intentioned, only reinforce that perception.

Despite the events of 9/11, which were followed by a global outpouring of sympathy and outrage, recent events around the world make clear that millions and millions of people perceive the U.S. as an enemy. This has not happened by accident: the current Republican administration has alienated much of the world by pursuing an imperial foreign policy while heavy-handedly repudiating international environmental and human-rights treaties. This administration has chosen not to acknowledge the need for the International Criminal Court, has refused to accept the Kyoto accords on global warming or the Land Mines treaty, and has decided to scrap the anti-ballistic missile treaty, to name but a few glaring instances of imperiousness.

It is shocking to realize that the U.S. has become the preeminent bully and rogue nation in the world, insisting on rules for others that we reject for ourselves.

When an honorable man like Colin Powell is forced to lie in public, when Mexicans at a soccer match against the U.S. chant "Osama," when our President has a less than 10 percent approval rating in much of Western Europe, when our one-time Shiite supporters in Karbala call George Bush's place "the Black House, not the White House," it's time for a change.

We badly need a president who can act as a true leader, someone who can once again serve as a role model for American values in the modern world. We need once again to see the U.S. championing policies that we the American people can be proud of as representative of our democratic values and convictions.

Among the principles that will be embraced by the next Democratic administration are a worldwide reduction in weapons of mass destruction, the re-empowering of the United Nations as the appropriate venue for addressing international concerns, a commitment to a world community of nations, and an understanding that progressive economic globalization is in the best interests of all the world's citizens.

The new administration will dedicate itself to the establishment of a democratic, socially just, and environmentally sustainable global economy. If the U.S. is to remain a leader in this global economy, we can ask no less of ourselves than to promote such values. That commitment must, and will, include an acknowledgment that policies that serve only the interests of large corporations contribute to political instability and therefore invite terrorism as a response.

In tangible demonstration of its commitment to world peace, the United States will take concrete steps to reverse the proliferation of weapons of mass destruction. These steps will include participation in multinational police actions to stamp out the clandestine worldwide trade in weapons and weapons technology, as well as steps to reduce U.S. stocks of such weapons and the programs for their development and manufacture. In fiscal year 2005 and beyond, weapons research and development funds will be reallocated to fund international programs to detect, track, and interdict production and transport of weapons of mass destruction.

The United Nations is rooted in the United States. It was founded in San Francisco more than fifty years ago, and is headquartered in New York. We believe it is vital to the world's future to rebuild and strengthen this institution, not as a tool of U.S. foreign policy but as a truly multinational entity. If the world is to survive, it will be because the nations of the world have learned how to grow together rather than having succumbed to the seductive but ultimately destructive appeals of nationalism and ethnic and religious divisiveness. As the Democratic Party noted four years ago, "America has a responsibility to lead, and should lead from within the international community." The Republican Party has in the past four years failed miserably at this. A new, clear-sighted leader is needed.

Even setting aside the many diplomatic arguments in favor of multinationalism, there is one undeniable economic argument: The United States, rich though it is, cannot afford to run the world. We lack the resources to police a whole planet. (As events in Iraq have demonstrated, we lack the expertise as well.) Only the international community can do that.

If our leaders insist on expending our human and material resources on wars to enforce our policies, we will exhaust our resources and leave ourselves and future generations far more vulnerable than we were before. We also will squander international good will and forfeit the support of other nations, as happened with our ill-fated incursion into Iraq after 9/11. Inevitably, we will create more enemies than we neutralize, making preventive war a sure path to national bankruptcy and the decline and fall of the U.S. There are, ultimately, many more of "them" than there are of "us," and their desperation is so much greater than ours. As Secretary of Defense Donald Rumsfeld himself fretted, "The cost-benefit ratio is against us. Our cost is billions against the terrorists' costs of millions. Madrasas and radical clerics are recruiting, training, and deploying terrorists faster than the United States can kill or capture them."

To claim that the war in Iraq was intended to fight terrorism is as false and disingenuous as to say that its aim was to liberate to Iraqi people from a cruel dictator (or, as some Europeans have joked, to rid the world of all cruel dictators starting with the letter "S").

The so-called "war to liberate Iraq" has actually made us more vulnerable rather than safer from terrorist attacks in three important ways.

First of all, our country's posture has inflamed the Arab world and bred a whole new generation of terrorists. It will take at least *another* generation to undo this damage. While Saddam Hussein was a horrific tyrant and the world is happier without him, we give the appearance of selectively overthrowing one brutal dictator whose removal happened to be our President's personal obsession, even before his taking office, and whose removal also served his corporate supporters' objectives in providing reconstruction contracts in an oil-rich nation.

Secondly, the Iraq War and Occupation have expended

enormous resources, almost 200 billion dollars at this point, money that could have gone into homeland security and direct military and Special Forces action and intelligence to interdict terrorists. We presently have a government that has made us less safe internationally while spending enormous sums of money and expending our national resources in claiming to make us more safe. Resources are being funneled into an almost bottomless pit, where they will continue to dissipate until we get international aid in restoring Iraqi governance and integrity. The construction of a new American empire not only is a betrayal of our founding principles, but a path that leads to bankruptcy.

Thirdly, we have damaged longstanding coalitions, alienated key allies throughout the world, and undermined global cooperation on terrorism.

The next administration will inherit a fragile and destabilized Iraq and must participate in protecting and stabilizing it, reestablishing multilateralism and the moral as well as political and economic mandate of the UN. There will be no choice, and this administration, having depleted our respect and influence in the international community, is in no position to regain a seat of leadership or moral authority. The entire world, not just the United States, urgently needs a new administration in Washington. The alternative is to allow Iraq to fall into chaos and become a terrorist base for the Middle East and the planet.

Despite the administration's assertion that the war in Iraq was meant to bring democracy to the Middle East, there was no plan in place for how to do this, not even a minimal road map for initiating the process. If Saddam Hussein's brutal mode of governing kept order in Iraq and prevented civil war and anarchy, what improvement can we offer in its stead, either for Iraqi or American security? Unfortunately the war's planners have been making it up as they go along. The administration waged a professional war because it had access to a well-financed, well-trained military developed by previous administrations, and then followed its conquest with an amateurish attempt to impose a peace. In the process, it has squandered decades of defense funding and strategic augmentation, and dramatically weakened the military itself. Every new attack on our troops in Iraq erodes our capacity to defend ourselves, diminishes our stature in the world, undermines our morale, and, despite the Defense Department's parameter of "acceptable casualties," sacrifices the actual lives and futures of many wonderful young men and women—their potential as human beings, what they might have contributed to society, and our investment in their training.

In practical terms, Iraqi occupation means an indefinite period of exposing our troops to freelance Jihadism on foreign turf. We have put our country and our young men and women right on the target line in al-Qaeda's shooting gallery, with little strategic gain from it.

Every problem that is soluble by weaponry is soluble by diplomacy. It is often more difficult, but it is more likely to stay solved.

The "War" on Terrorism

The "War on Terror" is a piece of outright demagoguery, a distraction, a persuasive bogeyman that allows the Bush administration to pursue its true aspiration—unabashed domination of the world's dwindling resources and an equally audacious abridgment of the inconvenient Bill of Rights.

The unspeakable mass murders committed on September 11, 2001, were crimes against humanity. No civilized state can countenance the murders of thousands of innocent citizens, and we must cooperate in bringing the perpetrators to justice.

It is important to recognize that the United States is not the sole target of these criminals. Globalization has transformed the international order that defined the 20th century. Today, the destinies of billions of people around the world are intertwined, and our domestic and international challenges are bound together as never before.

We have every right to defend ourselves, and our policies are tough and uncompromising. We mean to fight terrorists and terrorism throughout the globe. We will defend ourselves. Period. When threatened, we will disrupt plans and disable as many of those who would do us harm as we can, wherever they are, before they can strike at us. In fact, we are more efficient and less distracted at this task than the party that has been in power, for we do not confuse private agendas and political aggrandizement with the job of protecting our country.

We believe the campaign against terrorism is misconceived as a "war." It should be, instead, a massive multifaceted campaign to make the world a safer place—a campaign in which armed forces have an important but not sole central role. With our allies, we must maintain vigilance, eliminate havens where those with deadly intent can hide, seek out criminal perpetrators, and foreclose all possibilities of access to weapons of mass destruction. For the sake of all our futures, this must be a multi-national campaign. There are pragmatic as well as principled reasons why the rest of the world must be equally involved, as the many missteps that have surfaced during the current administration's clumsy attempts to play world policeman make clear.

"Terror" does not develop in a vacuum. The diplomatic and economic policies that the United States pursues affect people around the globe and influence perceptions of our country among other cultures. To the extent that we are seen as empire-builders, as the defenders of an oppressive status quo, as supporters of colonialism or as religious crusaders, we imperil our country and expose its citizens as targets, and all the might of U.S. forces will not prevent significant casualties. We think that if the policies pursued by the current administration change, the anger driving attacks against the U.S. will gradually diminish.

At the same time, when many ordinary people throughout the world are so angry and desperate that they threaten violence, it makes sense to figure out what they are angry about. We can and must strike back where possible and appropriate, but at the same time, surely at the very least we ought to listen to and try to understand what they are saying and why. It is a much wiser choice to change policies that are generating rage and revenge fantasies than to try to kill every young man and woman inspired to terrorism by them.

With each indulgent military attack, boast, and dare, the Republican administration enrages and incites more and more Muslims. Remember: they number a billion. Sooner or later they will find their Saladin, one more charismatic and dangerous than Osama bin Laden. When he unites them and focuses on the United States, we will regret the policies of bullying, preemption, unilateralism, and righteous imperiousness presently so dear to Republican campaigners boasting that we have been made safer by their bold actions.

The odd use of the word "terror" in place of "terrorism" by the President and members of his administration is a telling betrayal of the tongue. They do not readily distinguish between the primal terror that is rooted in poverty and vulnerability, on the one hand, and the retaliatory political act of injuring and terrorizing people, on the other. Terror is a fundamental human response to terrifying and terrible conditions; it cannot be attacked, except by eliminating the conditions that create it. Even "terrorism" itself is too broad an enemy. "Terrorism" is a tactic, and one can't make war on a tactic. Only those who attack us or plan to do so, by terrorism or other means, are our enemies. No one else. A "war on terrorism," as we have seen, too easily becomes a blank check to attack anyone the attacker chooses.

To label those whom the administration chooses to battle as evil-doers and suggest that we are combating "terror" sets America up in almost comic-book terms as the defender of freedom and democracy against an irrational force with which there can be no sane discussion or rational compromise. As the administration poses the situation, the only option is to annihilate them. By repeating this mantra while hiding its own agenda, the Bush team has stripped the terrorist attacks on the U.S. of their real political significance and made them nothing more than the cruel and depraved acts of bloodthirsty Islamic fanatics who are jealous of our freedoms and whose main ambition in life is to kill Americans and go to paradise as martyrs.

Note the al-Qaeda message after the Madrid bombings: "Stop targeting us, release our prisoners, and leave our land; we will stop attacking you. The people of U.S. allied countries have to put pressure on their governments to immediately end their alliance with the U.S. in the war on Islam. If you persist we will continue." The leader of al-Qaeda said at the time of the 9/11 attacks that he did not want Americans to sleep in peace and comfort as long as Muslims couldn't. Although we do not sanction terrorists setting our agendas and policies, and despite their unconscionable slaughter of innocents to make their point, this is a straightforward political declaration, not the raving of a band of fanatical zealots who "hate our freedoms," as President Bush keeps sloganizing.

More broadly, we must ask why the U.S. supports dictatorships and the corporate plunder of other peoples' resources, and whether these are policies we wish to embrace.

The coming Democratic administration must be an opportunity to re-evaluate on a case-by-case basis, to ask whether we wish to continue policies that enrich our country at others' expense.

Even if we set principle aside, we cannot embrace a pessimistic view of humanity and still expect to survive—there simply will be too many "evil-doers" to contain, and ultimately they will overwhelm us. Led by a new administration, the United States must instead presume that despite varied and different interests, all humanity shares common human dreams. If we act on that belief and make it possible for other people to determine their own destinies, rather than actively hindering their attempt to do so, they will eventually stop targeting us as the enemy and instead see us as fellow world citizens.

In addition to being largely ineffectual in protecting us against terrorist acts, the policies being pursued by the current administration threaten our civil liberties and many of the qualities of democracy that make the United States the unique entity that it is. In particular, we reject and will work for the repeal of the so-called "Patriot" acts and associated pieces of legislation, which are scatter-shot attempts to limit our constitutional freedoms in order to make it easier for government agents to conduct surveillance and the monitoring of lawful activities within our borders.

A Democratic administration will conduct the policing of the United States and defense of its peoples from attacks using policies that emphasize cooperation among law enforcement agencies and strategic surveillance and enforcement. We believe that security and liberty can coexist. No one, whether citizen or foreign national, will be deprived of the rights guaranteed by the U.S. Constitution and international law, nor will those rights be diminished in the name of national security.

We reject the presumed-guilty approach taken by this administration toward individuals it chooses to detain or question. Under a Democratic administration, the government will not jail individuals without legal representation or hold them for indefinite periods without making specific charges or bringing them to trial. The laws of this country will not be abrogated on the excuse of protection from terrorism.

None of these reaffirmations of our constitutional principles will diminish our determination to bring to justice those who have harmed our fellow citizens and attacked our soil. We believe that tracking down international criminals will proceed more quickly and effectively if pursued through international cooperation and freed of partisan political agendas.

It will proceed *most* effectively, though, if our government first identifies what its goals are. Declaring that we are waging a "war on terrorism" tells us, our legislators, and our armed forces nothing. We believe that if we are going to divert significant national resources to a campaign against terrorism, and even send our young men and women into battle, we must first understand and develop a national consensus on who or what we are fighting, what our goals are, and what a reasonable yardstick for measuring success would be.

The current administration's domestic security priorities puzzle us. Two and a half years after 9/11, fire departments still do not have enough radios for half their firefighters, and two-thirds of U.S. firehouses are short-staffed. Despite its rhetoric, the Bush administration has pursued an agenda that is little more than a shoulder-shrug—attacks are inevitable and no one can protect every locale at all times. This agenda appears to be more about the president's reelection than the safety and security of 280 million Americans. The Democratic administration's priority is to prepare local fire and police departments with the equipment, technology, and staff to develop means of preventing and dealing with terrorist attacks.

Foreign Policy

The containment of evil-doers is a preposterous concept. The attempt to pursue a foreign policy that is really a thinly disguised strategy of boosting U.S. corporations at the expense of the economic well-being of the rest of the world is equally short-sighted and ludicrous. It is time for the United States to commit itself to a true brotherhood of nations, and to do so with a full understanding that effective globalization will inevitably have consequences for a country that consumes a disproportionate share of the world's resources.

The United States need not look far for a simple, all-encompassing yardstick to guide our foreign policy. Our Declaration of Independence states, "We hold these truths to be self-evident, that all men are created equal." *All* men—in today's usage, *all* men and women. This is a universal declaration, one that does not restrict itself to U.S. citizens, or Caucasians, or Christians, or those who speak English. It extends to all peoples beyond our national borders. If we mean what we have for decades said, they are equals, not children to be ruled over for their own good. They cannot be classified as suited or unsuited for democracy at our changing convenience, and their countries ought not to be subject to our occupation. Their civic order certainly should not be deformed in the name of our supposed "strategic" needs.

We consider any foreign policy that is based on such a double standard to be a betrayal of our founding principles and to be profoundly un-American.

In that light, we will pursue the following policy realignments:

The Middle East

The United States should declare, and act on, its determination to support an international initiative to establish two democratic states encompassing Palestine.

We propose an immediate halt to Israeli settlement activity in the West Bank and a sequential dismantling of existing settlements; a cessation of Israeli construction of a fence separating them from the Palestinians and its rapid removal; an end to military occupation of the West Bank and Gaza; and a reexamination of Israeli policies of expropriating land and water from Palestinian communities.

We believe that all questions relating to this conflict, including the status of Jerusalem and the rights of the Palestinians dispossessed from their homes in 1948, need to be resolved in accordance with international principles of justice and all existing United Nations resolutions, rather than according to the asymmetry of power between the two parties.

We embrace as a model for Mideast peace the recently

proposed Geneva Accord. The Preamble of the Accord makes several important points. It affirms a determination by both sides to live in peaceful coexistence, mutual dignity, and security based on a just, lasting, and comprehensive peace and on achieving a historic reconciliation. It affirms the right of both the Jewish people and the Palestinian people to statehood, while asserting that within each state, minority populations are entitled to equal rights with the majority. And it calls for this document to be the first step toward true reconciliation and peaceful relations between the Arab world and Israel.

This proposed agreement provides that Israel and Palestine recognize each other as the homelands of their respective peoples. They agree to cooperate with each other and to work with the international community to maximize the benefit of peace to their respective populations. Palestine will consist of all of the West Bank and Gaza; the land that Palestine cedes to Israel will be matched by ceding of equal amount of land by Israel to Palestine. Israel will resettle the Israeli settlers from Palestinian sovereign territory while leaving intact immovable property, which will be transferred to Palestinian sovereignty.

A corridor will be established linking the West Bank and Gaza. The permanently open corridor will be under Israeli sovereignty and Palestinian administration; it will be surrounded by defensive barriers to prevent Palestinians from entering Israel through this corridor or Israelis from entering Palestine.

Palestine and Israel will each refrain from the threat or use of force against the territorial integrity or political independence of the other, and refrain from joining or assisting any coalition or alliance whose objective is to launch acts of hostility against the other. Each will prevent the formation of armed bands or mercenaries and militias in their respective territories and will disband all such existing groups.

Both sides will work together to build a secure and stable Middle East free from weapons of mass destruction. Palestine will not have an army. A multi-national force will be established to provide security for the Palestinian state (and indirectly for Israel). This force will protect the territorial integrity of the state of Palestine and help in the enforcement of anti-terrorism measures.

Jerusalem will become the capital of two states. Palestine will have sovereignty over East Jerusalem, and Israel will have sovereignty over West Jerusalem. A multi-national presence will maintain the security of the Temple Mount, to prevent digging, excavation, or construction on the Compound and to ensure that it will not be used for any hostile acts against Israelis or Israeli areas. The Wall will be under

Israeli sovereignty, and the Compound will be under the sovereignty of Palestine.

Refugees will be entitled to compensation for their refugee status and for their loss of property, and states that have hosted Palestinian refugees have the right to remuneration. The refugees will have a choice of permanent place of residence: Palestine, their present host country, third countries, or Israel (but Israel will be the sole determiner of how many refugees to accept).

Israelis may be granted permits for use of designated roads through Palestine. Israel and Palestine will establish special arrangements to guarantee access to agreed-upon sites of religious significance.

American funds will not support Israeli military activity at the expense of the Palestinians. The U.S. will support instead the development of a regional economic zone that makes use of the resources and talents of all in the region. Moreover, we must review our relationship with Israel to understand where the U.S.'s long-term interests lie. If we are to embrace and defend a strategic relationship with Israel, the citizens of this country deserve to understand in what ways it benefits us. If we do not, on what basis and for what benefits are we to justify being at war with the whole Arab world? As our first president, George Washington, wrote in his Farewell Address:

"A passionate attachment of one nation for another produces a variety of evils. Sympathy for the favorite nation, facilitating the illusion of an imaginary common interest in cases where no real common interest exists, and fusing into one the enmities of the other, betrays the former into a participation in the quarrels and wars of the latter without adequate inducement and justification. It leads also to concessions to the favorite nation of privileges denied to others which is apt doubly to injure the nation making the concessions; by unnecessarily parting with what ought to have been retained, and by exciting jealousy, ill-will, and a disposition to retaliate, in the parties from whom equal privileges are withheld."

North Korea

North Korea is the last of the post-World War II Stalinist states. Its economy is in shambles, yet it maintains a million-man army—one of the world's strongest and most war-ready—facing 40,000 American troops across the Demilitarized Zone. Formally, the Korean War has not ended, having only been fought to a standstill and truce in 1953.

The new Democratic administration will bring the North Korean crisis to an end. In return for North Korea eliminating its nuclear weapons and ballistic missile programs, the U.S. will begin to normalize relations. The easing of trade sanctions is critical to North Korea, which has suffered devastating food shortages and severe famine.

The new U.S. government will make the Geneva Accord of 1994 the cornerstone of a new U.S. policy toward North Korea. Its Agreed Framework Between the United States of America and the Democratic People's Republic of Korea represented the first time that the U.S. officially recognized the validity of the DPRK's security interests and economic needs. Even in the face of North Korea's exorbitant militarization and strategic starvation of its own people, we must restrain our outrage and reinforce the sincerity of our 1994 recognition. To rail publicly against Kim Jong Il's despotic, megalomaniac cult is facile and permissive, yielding "Axis of Evil" sound bites but little of value to anyone, particularly the oppressed within Korea.

We cannot change North Korea overnight. But, while conceding that a military solution is always available (though as a horrible last resort), we can change the Bush administration's empty policy of confrontation. Trying to coerce North Korea into becoming a more democratic, less militarized society is futile, a rhetorical gambit embraced more for its domestic propaganda value than its potential to deliver results. If the U.S.'s goal is to reduce tensions in Southeast Asia and lessen the danger of nuclear proliferation, we should cease threatening and moralizing and instead reassure the North Korean government that we intend no coup or invasion.

This is a serious crisis with potentially catastrophic consequences for North Korea's neighbors, but it is also a crisis that skillful diplomacy could quickly diffuse. Kim Jong Il, a fan of American pop culture and cinema, has made his position quite clear, labeled it for us, and telegraphed all his punches. He wants to trade his weapons and nuclear program for security guarantees and economic aid. President Bush and his advisors don't like this deal, so they choose not to engage in the necessary asymmetric diplomacy. Instead they seem content to play the dumb, belligerent bad cop to Kim's mad dictator, reacting to his taunts without irony, daring him to deadlier actions.

The U.S. should place the normalization of diplomatic and economic relations with the DPRK on a fast track, combining the bilateral approach favored by North Korea with the U.S. multilateral approach in simultaneous negotiations. The result, a normalized relationship, would provide Washington with more leverage to press for changes in North Korea and inevitably lead to a more open society.

As the normalization process begins, the U.S. government should work with the DPRK to:

- Transform the armistice agreement into a peace treaty.

- Reduce levels of conventional troops near the demilitarized zone.
- End DPRK exports of Scud B and C missiles and missile technology.
- Repatriate the remains of U.S. MIA soldiers.

Washington should gradually lift economic sanctions (in place since 1953) to facilitate North Korea's goal of ending its isolation, improving socioeconomic conditions, and slowly opening sectors of its economy to the international market. It is now time for the U.S., in concert with South Korea, China, and Japan, to use the carrot of improved economic and diplomatic relations to help shape better relations between North and South Korea.

Cuba

In knee-jerk pursuit of an outmoded policy of opposition to an anachronistic ideology, the United States unnecessarily has visited decades of hardship on the Cuban people. We believe the re-establishment of full diplomatic and economic ties with Cuba will do more to modernize that island state and improve the condition of its people than four decades of blockade has done. And even before the outrageous use of the U.S. base at Guantanamo Bay as an extra-constitutional prison camp sharpened our resolve, we have believed that the continued insistence on this occupation of Cuban territory is unnecessary, and emblematic of an era in U.S. foreign policy that ought long ago to have ended.

The President as World Leader

We reject the jingoistic style adopted by George W. Bush. We are offended by the manner in which he has conducted himself upon the world stage. What the President and his cronies are trumpeting as "strength and confidence" is actually hubris and swagger from armchair warriors. The next chief executive of the United States and his Cabinet and advisors will comport themselves with dignity and, in the absence of any reason to act otherwise, with respect toward other sovereign countries and their peoples. In speaking to the world, representing the American people, the president's actions will be informed by an awareness of the vast injustices and suffering experienced throughout the world, much of it caused by U.S. economic agendas. His statements will reflect a recognition that many of those who have declared themselves America's enemies are fighting against the loss of their lands and cultures in the only way they know or that is available to them. While true terrorists must be fought with every resource at the United States' disposal, there need be no boasting, daring, or saber-rattling activities that, as we have noted, only increase America's vulnerability and enhance its attractiveness as a target for enemies.

U.S. Armed Forces

The United States requires uniformed troops to ensure its security. But the substantial size of our Armed Forces distorts the federal budget and increases the deficit, making it easy to brand non-military programs as unaffordable. Not only personnel but also dollars flow overseas to support the military, both directly and indirectly. Finally, it is obvious that Americans in military uniforms have served as targets for those who feel oppressed by the U.S.

This presidential campaign offers the opportunity to discuss anew the size of our Armed Forces and what roles the people who wear those uniforms should play. What are the pros and cons of having bases around the world? What should the balance be between forces in active service and the Reserves and National Guard?

The transparent connection between national security and international relations requires the U.S. military to be combat-effective while playing a peace-supporting role by creating and maintaining strategic friendships and alliances in an often hostile world. A military that is defined simply as a technological sword to be used to support imperialistic and expansionist goals inevitably will alienate cultural, ethnic, and religious groups, creating the potential or increasing the likelihood that they will become enemies overseas and in our own backyard. At the same time, if we do not maintain a military that can act quickly and forcefully, we will be seen as weak, unprepared, and easily exploited.

A humane, strong, and balanced policy toward our military will include the following:

- We will run the military like a business. This means reducing the current massive bureaucratic infrastructure to make the military more mobile and agile. This can cut the military budget without impacting effectiveness.
- We will increase Special Operations as a proportion of our armed forces and improve its training, so our government has at its disposal a force that is both light and lethal. This is necessary where the priority is to deal with small groups of insurgents rather than Cold War-style conventional forces. We note that it took only 440 Special Operations soldiers (many of them on horseback) to bring down the Taliban regime in Afghanistan. Efficient and mobile ground forces are essential when an invasion is required.
- We will reduce the number of conventional troops.

- We will create a cadre of warrior-diplomats, middle-level officers, and senior NCOs who can, while operating with minimal infrastructure and support, engender positive relationships in far-away places. Building friendships in this way is extremely effective. This will be a concrete expression of the approach that we mean to embrace: make friends and cultivate relationships from a place of strength.
- We will develop a military training regimen that actually *trains* civil affairs units instead of putting them together, *ad hoc,* when needed. Like it or not, Operations Other than War are here to stay. Conflict resolution, community building, health services, mediation, training local police forces and militia, and building infrastructure (water, sanitation, electricity, education) are all tasks appropriate for a civil affairs Special Operations unit.
- We will build into the training process a character-development regimen that is influenced by latest research in learning and values embodiment, much like the new Marine Corps Martial Arts Program (MCMAP). The martial-arts section, while effective on deployment and liberty, is equally a delivery system for character values. This also prepares young men and women to be exemplary citizens when they leave the service.

We also want to explore possible models that, if adopted, might encourage a broader volunteerism. Envision, for example, a Department of Peace that trains people in nonviolent conflict resolution with the goal of service to the planet as well as to the population within America's boundaries. We believe the next administration should consider reviving the Peace Corps as a tool for developing and deepening sociocultural links with other countries.

Weapons Systems

Committed to strength with flexibility, the next administration will reexamine all existing and planned weapons systems in the context of the world we find ourselves in. Among the candidates for elimination are the B-1 and B-2 bombers, the F-14A, F-14D and F-15 fighter jets, the Aegis air-defense cruiser, the Patriot missile system, the M-1 Abrams tank, the MX missile, and all satellite-based weaponry and missile-defense systems.

The need for this reexamination is undeniable. Patriot missiles shot down almost as many "friendly" pilots as enemy missiles during the Gulf and Iraq wars, yet the military has downplayed or concealed such failures, preferring to give the impression that what clearly are fundamental flaws in weaponry were merely developmental problems to be ironed out.

Bad weapons systems—ratified by falsified tests, paid for by inflating military budgets, and protected by military careerists defending their turf—lead to catastrophic consequences: the deaths of soldiers, a false sense of security, and a devastating waste of money. We will evaluate military technologies for their true usefulness and weed out weapons systems that protect only profits, careers, and budgets within the military-industrial complex.

Overseas Bases

The presence of U.S. bases in nearly 100 countries poses a huge problem for the world and for us. For much of its existence our country was a City on the Hill for the world to look at and imitate. Today, though, beyond TV and movies (which are problematic enough), much of the world knows us as the proprietors of military bases—gated private communities with bowling alleys, movie theaters, playing fields, and a population of bored eighteen-year-olds with too much time on their hands.

Most overseas U.S. military bases were built during the Cold War. The Cold War now is over, yet our government maintains these bases, many of dubious strategic value, at enormous cost in a time of drastic budget cuts. Supporters defend these bases using questionable arguments, such as their ability to provide essential refueling points and listening posts for vital electronic intelligence relevant to the war on terror. In fact, though, technology has rendered these bases obsolete for anything other than staging points for preemptive strikes. We note that one of the reasons Osama bin Laden gave for attacking us on 9/11 was the presence of U.S. bases in Saudi Arabia.

We believe it is time for a thorough, impartial, cost-benefit analysis of all these bases.

Intelligence Agencies

The embarrassing failure of U.S. intelligence agencies to assess Iraq's weaponry accurately is only the latest example in a long history of wasted resources and the perversion of the government's high-powered intelligence apparatus for political ends. The failure to know what is really going on and the invention of "truth" to justify political policies determined in advance must end.

We therefore call for the restructuring of the executive branch and military intelligence agencies. The twin goals must be to improve accuracy and to reduce the potential for political influence on the intelligence gathering and reporting process. We support the creation of a management-level intelligence review board, with appointees chosen from retired intelligence officers with distinguished records of service and a history of having spoken out against abuses in the past. This panel will be charged to review and vet the intelligence being provided to the executive branch.

The Central Intelligence Agency is badly in need of reform. We do not presume to know what the best structure ought to be—determining that should be the task of an independent bi-partisan commission—but we are sympathetic to two proposals: to spin off the government's covert operations units into an independent agency that needs signed presidential and congressional approval to undertake aggressive action, and to give the analysis units political independence by appointing the director of central intelligence for a long fixed period (probably ten years), as now is done with the FBI director.

Crime

As the party noted in its 2000 Platform, Democrats believe that government's most basic duty is to establish law, order, and freedom and to keep citizens safe from crime. "When crime is rampant, families are forced off the streets and behind closed doors. When children are ducking for cover, they have a hard time reaching for their dreams. When people are afraid to walk in their own neighborhood, communities are robbed of the basic sense of decency and togetherness."

Many of the goals enumerated in that platform are still to be achieved. In the face of intense pressure on local budgets, we must still increase the number of community police on our streets. We must still reform a justice system that is badly broken, spilling far too many prisoners back onto our streets each year addicted to drugs, unrehabilitated, and primed to commit another crime. (See "Prison Reform.")

As a nation, we must invest in front-end solutions to crime. Quality after-school programs, child care, and targeted at-risk youth and parent programs are far more cost-effective strategies for reducing crime and violence than building more prisons. The link between failing in school and incarceration is so well established that only a foolish or ideologically blinded administration would resist larger investments in targeted educational programs.

We also must join the community of civilized nations in finally eliminating the death penalty, a failed deterrent that stains us all. The policy of "an eye for an eye" leaves everyone blind; it becomes one more grotesque public spectacle, one more reality show for those inured to real human suffering and its costs. When we eradicate these husks of human beings in cruel, maudlin ceremonies, we lose all chance of rehabilitation, all chance of redemption, and all chance to learn something about what it was that committed the deed and then vacated, and we implicate and brutalize our whole society.

We cannot teach our young that it is wrong to kill by killing, nor ought we to walk away from the responsibility to help heal those among us who have been injured to the point where they choose to take life. It is our responsibility to leave this Earth and the societies upon it better than we found them; we cannot do that by burying the challenges to our societal norms.

The War on Drugs

Addictive drugs are epidemic in our poor neighborhoods, in large measure because they allow an escape from a day-to-day reality that otherwise seems inescapable, and because selling drugs on the streets is one of the very few ways that those with otherwise unmarketable skills can make money. For someone with a family to support, the choice to sell drugs for earnings comparable to those of a young corporate executive rather than compete for a minimum-wage, minimum-status job with a fast food chain or its equivalent is no choice at all.

Of the country's 2 million prisoners, 450,000 are incarcerated in prison or jail for drug offenses—more people than the European Union, an entity with 100 million more people, has in prison for *all crimes combined.* The 450,000 figure underestimates the role that the "war on drugs" plays in the use of incarceration in the country: studies have shown that about a third of America's prisoners tested positive for drugs or alcohol at the time of their offense.

Unless we deal with serious drug addiction as a disease, and occasional recreational and medical drug use (notably involving marijuana) as a non-criminal lifestyle choice (like alcohol or cigarettes), we are choosing an inflexible, regimented, almost medieval society—superstitious, randomly and gratuitously punitive, and obsessed with moralistic retribution. We are also giving organized crime and gangs throughout the country a perfect opportunity, a ready-made product to exploit.

Meanwhile, the spread of drugs has become a severe economic, law-enforcement, community, and even military issue at a time when outside terrorists are looking to buy inside collaborators. While obsessing about punishing the victims—those who threaten us least—the Republicans are ignoring a grave threat to their own constituencies. Dangerous drugs and their accomplices, crimes and decrepitude, are spreading like the diseases they are from urban hubs to the economically devastated heartland. Whole towns in Wyoming, the Dakotas, the deep South, even parts of New England have been devastated by a cycle of decay that includes as key elements debilitating drug use and drug violence. Drugs beget many victims—people who should be offered not punishment but treatment on demand, a way out and a viable alternative. Punishment should be reserved for those who import and wholesale those drugs.

The "war on drugs," which has consumed billions of dollars in policing, court, prison, and community costs, has been a dismal failure. We must end this war by reallocating resources to improving access to and effectiveness of drug treatment programs for the millions of people who need them, and by treating the serious drug problems that are at the base of the criminality that leads so many to end up behind bars. California, Texas, Arizona, and Kansas have recently changed laws to allow more addicted prisoners to receive drug treatments in their communities rather than in prison cells. Government policy must be changed to decriminalize marijuana and other relatively mild recreational and health-oriented drugs and to emphasize treatment over incarceration, particularly in the prison system where more than half of the inmates are drug offenders.

Gun Control

According to our Constitution, Americans have the right to bear arms for the defense of our nation. However, common sense calls for appropriate licensing and monitoring of dangerous weapons so that they are not used for criminal purposes. As motor vehicles are regulated by the government to prevent their misuse and to ensure the responsibility of their owners, so should guns be licensed and registered.

Driven by right-wing zealots, Republicans have pursued the goal of making guns easier to get. We must oppose the attempts by these extremists and their allies in the gun industry to build immunity for gun makers into law. We also must reverse the weakening of the Brady Act forced through the Congress as part of the Omnibus Appropriations Bill. And we must make certain that the Congress re-authorizes the ban on the sale of assault weapons.

We support legislation to create a ballistic-fingerprinting system that would allow any bullet used in a criminal act to be traced back to a specific gun. With ballistic fingerprinting and appropriate background checks on all gun sales, we can give law-enforcement officials the tools they need to stop violent crimes by those using firearms.

Judges and the Supreme Court

President Bush has set out to pack the federal courts with judges appointed for life who embrace extreme judicial ideologies and will tilt the scales of justice for decades. The lineup of President Bush's proposed appellate appointees suggests the nature of the person that he is likely to propose to fill the next vacancy on the U.S. Supreme Court, which could develop soon after the election. No Supreme Court justice has retired in almost a decade, and both Chief Justice William Rehnquist and Justice Sandra Day O'Conner are believed to have expressed wishes to retire.

O'Connor's retirement in particular is crucial for the future of women's right to choose, since she is the swing vote protecting *Roe v. Wade.* Other issues that have been decided recently on 5-4 votes include the right of universities to use affirmative action programs to ensure diversity on their campuses, the limiting in scope of the Americans with Disabilities Act, the disenfranchisement of minority voters in Census Bureau counts, the limiting of workers' right to sue under the Fair Labor Standards Act, and the removal of Clean Water Act protection from one-fifth of the nation's wetlands.

We support a judicial-appointment process free of the taint of ideologues. We demand a president who will appoint to the U.S. Supreme Court justices who have a demonstrated concern for and commitment to the individual rights protected by our Constitution, including the right to privacy.

II. IN SEARCH OF ENDURING PROSPERITY

George W. Bush has presided over the unraveling of the striking social and economic gains of the New Deal era. That era, suspended between two world wars and encompassing an economic depression to which an activist Democratic administration responded forcefully, yielded as one of its legacies a significant narrowing of the income gaps among Americans.

The egalitarian reforms that were born in the New Deal endured for decades. But no more. They now are dying the death of a thousand cuts.

Over the last thirty years the real income of the bottom 90 percent of American taxpayers actually fell—by 7 percent, according to one report—while the income (not the capital gains, just the income) of the top 1 percent rose by almost 150 percent. More to the point, the income of the top 0.1 percent rose by almost 350 percent, and the income of the top 0.01 percent rose by close to 600 percent.

This is not an accident. It is a deliberate strategy, the most recent gambits of which were three years of regressive tax cuts forced through by the Bush administration to benefit its supporters among the very rich and many large businesses. As Al Sharpton has noted, "What we have is a selective recovery for the rich."

The majority of Americans do not support this strategy. We take a very different view of the economy and the responsibility of the United States government toward its citizens and the rest of the world.

In fact, we even differ with most politicians about the appropriate time frame within which to consider needed economic reforms. A platform focused on a four-year electoral term inevitably relies too heavily on short-term thinking. But this short-term approach, and the associated failure to factor in long-term consequences, threatens the future of the Earth and all who live upon it.

As responsible citizens and political people, we therefore must challenge ourselves to embrace a longer-term perspective and convince skeptics that this is the wisest course.

Wealth, Taxes, and the Role of Government

The Bush administration has pursued economic policies that increased the stratification of U.S. society and widened the gap between the relative haves and have-nots. It has eliminated the estate tax, after waging a duplicitous campaign to convince U.S. taxpayers that the repeal would have broad impact when it fact it benefited only a small number of very wealthy taxpayers. It has reduced tax rates on corporate profits and on unearned income. It has increased the number of tax shelters available only to the very rich, and broadly reduced tax rates for high-income taxpayers.

On the spending side, the administration's successive waves of tax cuts have created a fundamental imbalance between the federal government's revenues and its obligations to deliver services. Most immediately, this has meant that the government has been forced to reduce the availability of social welfare services and public and higher education for lower-income citizens. More broadly, the path this administration has embarked on will lead to huge and potentially destabilizing budget deficits, and ultimately to a massive dismantling of the New Deal social-safety-net programs: a sharp reduction in Social Security and unemployment benefits, the elimination of guaranteed useful medical coverage to older citizens under Medicare, and a similar contraction of Medicaid care for the poor.

Trustees for Medicare have now reported that this key U.S. health-care program for the elderly and disabled will have to start drawing money from its trust fund this year for the first time as expenditures outstrip incoming funds, fully seven years earlier than it forecast a year ago. The annual report from the government trustees forecasts that without changes, Medicare would become insolvent by 2019, twenty-three years earlier than the previous forecast for when it would go broke.

We reject the values and the view of the world that underlie this scheme to enrich Republican party cronies at the expense of most Americans. We do not accept the propaganda assertions that we all pay too much in taxes. The level of taxation of the U.S. middle class has not changed significantly in decades and is far lower than in many other developed countries.

Civilized societies provide services to their members through governments when such services can better be provided by governments than by private sources. Taxation creates the financial means to provide these services. In the words of former U.S. Supreme Court Justice Oliver Wendell Holmes Jr., "Taxes are what we pay for civilized society." The real problem is that the rich now pay far less in taxes than they have in the past. The highest tax rate currently is 35 percent, half what it was thirty years ago and, with one brief exception, the lowest rate since 1932. The effective tax rate on corporate profits has been cut in half since the 1960s. As Paul Krugman has noted, "By the time the Bush tax cuts have taken full effect, people with really high incomes will face their lowest average tax rate since the Hoover administration."

Tax savings for wealthy Americans do not translate into more revenue flowing through the country's institutions. They do not translate into more jobs, greater job security, or the improved well-being of the populace as a whole. In fact, they may even impact negatively those who are made wealthier, since the result of this situation inevitably will be a larger and more disaffected underclass and associated civil unrest. We are made less safe domestically by the widening of the gap between haves and have-nots and the creation of new jobless and homeless populations.

Rather than accept the cutting of social spending by as much as 40 percent—cuts that would drastically change the nature of the government services we want and have come to expect—we choose to retain the federal government's almost century-old commitment to the least advantaged among us and to reverse the current administration's anti-tax, shrink-government crusade. The new Democratic administration will embrace the principle of "From each according to his abilities, to each according to his needs," and will spearhead the drive to provide adequate funding for majoritarian government programs by increasing taxation of high-income individuals and families, unearned income, and corporate profits.

Specifically, tax rates should be returned to the pre-Reagan era maximum rate of 50 percent for the highest-income taxpayers. Sales taxes are regressive taxes that are needed to support local government, but they should again be deductible to eliminate the extra level of regressivity by not allowing a deduction from income tax for them. The 2 percent cutback on employee business expenses should be repealed. The tax treatment of legal settlements in which the plaintiff has hired an attorney on a contingent fee basis should be changed to tax the net settlement *after* deduction of the legal fee, rather than the gross settlement. Present treatment allowing the legal fee as a deduction is subject to so many limitations that the plaintiff often ends up with little or nothing after legal fees and income tax.

Tax preferences for the alternative minimum tax should be limited to items specific to high-income taxpayers. The preferences for tax and medical itemized deductions must be repealed. The preference for the capital gains portion of non-cash charitable contributions must be re-instituted. A new preference for contributions to pension plans in excess of $40,000 per year is called for. Preferences for depreciation in excess of actual diminution in value must be instituted.

In addition, to adjust one of the most regressive taxes, self-employment and Social Security taxes must not be income-limited. The inheritance tax will be reinstated, and a blue-ribbon commission will be appointed to develop legislative proposals for an equitable progressive taxation system that will be adequate to provide needed government services and to fund tax credits for small businesses and farms.

This will entail enacting a variety of disincentives for outsourcing jobs overseas, requiring companies to pay taxes on formerly tax-exempt foreign earnings, and rolling back tax breaks for companies that locate abroad. The Bush administration's recently created corporate loopholes, which cost approximately 100 billion tax dollars a year, must be closed by Congress. We need laws targeted specifically at recovering some of the estimated $50 billion of tax revenue lost annually as the result of corporate funds being sheltered in Panama, Belize, the U.S. Virgin Islands, Bahamas, and the Turks and Caicos Islands, among other locations.

The Bush administration is simply not telling the truth about the purpose or effect of its tax cuts. Because of their allegiances and their ideology, the Republicans are incapable of taking hoarded and surplus wealth from corporate coffers and restoring it to where it is needed: the funding of basic social programs in the areas of health care, education, housing, and homeland security; real job creation in communities; and deficit reduction. Instead, their approach to corporate taxation allows profits to move from one corporate pocket to another and ultimately to the bank accounts of the wealthiest Americans in the mistaken belief that democracy and freedom confer the right to make as much money as you can while impoverishing the society around you and disinheriting the working class and future Americans. In other words, they place the right to be rich above the right to have a job, a home, and a safe community. They know that not everyone will go along with this plan, so they disguise their agenda to make it seem that its benefits are greater, broader, and directed at all Americans.

Our administration will craft a plan to pay down the astronomical debt with which George W. Bush has saddled our children.

We reject the drive to privatize Social Security through the addition of individual accounts. Social Security is a critical social insurance program that has worked well for sixty years, is cost-effective, and has kept millions of retired Americans out of poverty. We recommend the financing and other changes to maintain Social Security's solvency advocated by Peter Diamond and Peter Orszag in their book, *Saving Social Security: A Balanced Approach.* We reject the recent costly changes to Medicare that do too little for those elderly Americans who are economically burdened by the high cost of drugs and do too much for HMOs and the drug industry. In fact, these changes are a brazen gift to the pharmaceutical companies disguised as a gift to senior citizens.

The Bush administration's economic standing appears to have benefited from the beginning of the long-hoped-for economic recovery. In the third quarter of 2003, the real Gross Domestic Product rose at an annual rate of 8.2 percent. But the pace of job creation lags behind, and wages remain flat; for that same period, wage and salary income, adjusted for inflation, rose at an annual rate of only 0.8 percent. What gains there have been show up in corporate profits, which rose at an annual rate of more than 40 percent in the third quarter. Since stock ownership is concentrated in the richest 5 percent of the population, with almost half of all the tax on corporate earnings paid by only 1 percent of the population, this is a recovery that is benefiting once again only a small minority of the population, the most affluent among us.

An administration that cannot generate jobs even as it generates improved corporate profits does not deserve the support of the vast majority of U.S. voters who are wage earners. A Democratic administration will reverse this situation through the development of both private- and public-sector employment programs, support for small and incubator businesses, and incentives to retain jobs within the U.S., as well as a progressive revision of the Tax Code.

The Power and Role of Corporations

It will require the next administration's first four-year term merely to agree on how to define and begin to publicly study the problem of corporate power in the U.S. It may well be that nothing will change within the lifetime of some of the readers of this document. But we refuse to accept that as a reason not to begin this exploration. A vote for the Republican candidate is a vote to continue the status quo, to deny that there is a problem with corporate power over our lives.

A vote for the Democratic candidate, on the other hand, is a vote for democracy. In a democracy, "we the people" constitute the only source of legitimate political power. It's time that we the people take our sovereignty as seriously as our forebears did and reassert our authority. A new administration committed to democratic principles and governance will stand up for the public interest rather than governance by and for corporations.

The rise of corporate power has been gradual, achieved through a very long series of incremental legal challenges, judicial decisions, and rewrites of laws. As a result, some Americans may have failed to grasp the magnitude of the hijacking of our political and economic institutions. Even more subtle, and more noteworthy, has been the colonization of our minds by corporate values. Like it or not, corporate values today define American culture.

That's because corporations wield inordinate power through the money they can spend and the property and constitutional rights they have arrogated to themselves. Ironically, while assuming the rights and protections afforded to "persons" under the U.S. Constitution, corporations benefit from a structure that absolves any individuals of legal responsibility for their actions.

The largest 300 corporations control about one-fourth of all the goods-producing assets in the world. The largest 100 have incomes greater than half the member countries of the United Nations. Today, giant corporations enter and leave communities at will, shaping the futures of people and ecosystems. Leaders of these corporations exercise sovereign control over vast lands (80 percent of all land used for export agriculture, for example) and mineral resources and innumerable species. They force local decisions, reshape cultural traditions, and affect regional ecologies and economies.

They also shape our lives by choosing, for reasons having little to do with the common welfare, how human beings are used as workers and which products and technologies are researched and created. They spend huge sums instructing us what values to embrace and what products to buy.

Such concentrated corporate power that can manipulate our democratic processes is contrary to the precepts that are supposed to shape governance in this nation. All power is supposed to be constitutional—that is, answerable to the people. Yet we the people have little legal or moral authority over giant corporations.

Reversing this trend and reducing corporate power will take some work. It will require some readjustment of our laws. But the key steps in taking back our government are simply two: We must elect candidates who are neither committed to the ideology of corporate governance nor beholden to the CEOs and board of directors of the Global 2,000; and we must demand the creation of a system of full public financing of election campaigns to remove the most obvious channel of corporate influence over our elected leaders. (See "Campaign Finance Reform.")

World Trade

Global trade today is shaped by "free trade" arrangements. The World Trade Organization (WTO) and treaties such as the North American Free Trade Agreement (NAFTA) and the Free Trade Area of the Americas (FTAA) may benefit importers and exporters, but they do so at the price of interfering with democratic governance worldwide. These agreements subvert laws enacted to protect human rights, workers' rights, jobs, and the environment. Trade rules set by corporate business interests in closed meetings allow them to challenge any local, state, or federal regulation that hurts profits, effectively usurping citizen sovereignty. NAFTA even allows foreign-owned companies to challenge our Constitution,

Congress, and our right to enact U.S. laws as "barriers" to their "free trade."

The ten-year-old NAFTA liberalized trade among Canada, Mexico, and the U.S. Under NAFTA, farmers' income in all three countries has declined, and millions of small farmers have lost their land due to devastating drops in commodity prices. Corporations involved in trade in international commodities, though, are reaping huge profits.

Not surprisingly, the NAFTA model doesn't address concentration of market share and profit in the hands of a few large corporations, or the ability of government-subsidized U.S. agribusiness to sell at prices below the cost of production. But despite the obvious instances of failure in the agricultural sector and elsewhere, new agreements are being modeled after NAFTA.

The FTAA is a trade agreement currently under negotiation that would expand NAFTA to every country in the hemisphere but Cuba. These negotiations lack meaningful public or Congressional input, but corporate interests are actively engaged.

It will be the policy of the next administration that rather than being expanded, NAFTA should be replaced with an international system of economic cooperation that fosters equality and community well-being. The new administration will explore the most effective approaches to repealing

NAFTA and withdrawing from the World Trade Organization. In its place, the U.S. will undertake to negotiate fair trade agreements that protect people, the environment, and the means of production.

Established in 1995 as the first permanent multilateral trade-negotiating forum, the WTO is today the most powerful legislative and judicial body on Earth, acting as a global enforcement mechanism for corporate-managed trade at the expense of all other interests. By promoting the free trade regime above the local interests of communities, working families, and the environment, the WTO has undermined democracy around the world. With WTO rules enforced by sanctions, the WTO's authority even eclipses national governments.

There is an alternative to the current corporation-serving world economy in which the drive for profits rules and small-scale producers are left out of the bargaining process. "Fair trade" is a sustainable model of international trade that guarantees fair prices and community empowerment. The new administration will support this viable and growing fair trade alternative to secret "free trade" negotiations.

To right a balance that has gone way off in the direction of corporate control and profits, international trade and investment must be viewed in the context of other societal goals such as economic justice, human rights, healthy communities, and a sound environment. A new administration will make fair-trade options available to American investors and consumers through education and government purchasing policy and will provide incentives for participation in fair trade arrangements.

The Economy and the Environment

According to a report from a Pentagon planning unit, climate change now poses a threat to global stability greater than that of terrorism. The document predicts that abrupt climate change could bring the planet to the edge of anarchy as countries develop nuclear capabilities to defend and secure dwindling food, water, and energy supplies.

In the light of such findings, and given the Bush administration's preoccupation with terrorism and demonstrated inclination to deny scientific data, it is imperative that the Democratic Party confront the issue of climate change immediately and fully.

Measures to reduce the environmental dangers we face are well known and proven. The umbrella strategy is to convert from a fossil fuel-based economy to one increasingly based on non-polluting renewable energies—solar, wind, small-scale hydroelectric, geothermal, and hydrogen-based.

(See "Energy.") The subsidies that prop up oil and coal have prevented this necessary conversion. To correct this, the Democratic Party must study the recommendations before the World Bank that would stop all funding of coal and oil development, increase renewable energy loans by 20 percent annually, and grant local peoples the right to veto energy development projects not in their best interests.

Automakers must drastically improve fuel efficiency and make available hybrid and hydrogen-powered vehicles. Additionally, agriculture, which is responsible for more than half the harmful chemicals impacting not only our air but our water supplies, needs to be fundamentally restructured. This must involve a rapid conversion to ecologically-based food production systems that include nutrient and greenhouse gas recycling and a sharp curtailment of industrialized and corporate farming, huge monocrop farms, and large-scale food transport. (See "Agriculture.")

In other words, the only way that the next and succeeding generations will inherit a planet on which humans can survive is for us to accelerate our steps along the path of conversion to sustainable development. Because of the scope and complexity of the problems and the long period needed for remediation, we cannot alter substantially the entire framework of the United States economy, and we should not in one grand gesture attempt to. However, we must acknowledge the need for this and understand what the journey must look like.

As a matter of long-term policy, the United States must agree to secure the involvement of the world's nations in treaties and cooperative programs to address the growing crises of water and air pollution, over-fishing, species extinction, global warming, the degradation of the Earth's ozone layer, overpopulation, deforestation, human-caused desertification and droughts, and other environmental degradations.

With the new Democratic administration in place, the United States will establish high-priority programs to preserve its own forests and bodies of water, to discourage conversion of farmland to commercial and residential purposes, and to halt the harvesting of old-growth timber. No new roads shall be constructed in wilderness areas.

The government must also take the lead in developing educational campaigns that emphasize the importance of renewable resources and the dangers and false promises of throwaway consumerism. Changing our country's economic values is a huge challenge, but our survival as a nation and ultimately as a species requires it: So long as we continue to consume, shape our climate, travel, and recreate in the ways that large corporations have conditioned us to, we will continue to invite our government to pursue policies that support those patterns and values. Challenging our consumerism is one of the key issues of the 21st century.

The President and Congress must strengthen and expand the responsibilities of the Environmental Protection Agency so that it becomes the lead agency for accomplishing environmental policy goals. One of the chief responsibilities of EPA officials will be to develop a tax and fee structure that will ensure that the environmental costs of pollution generation and the destruction of natural environments are charged to the companies engaged in such practices as a cost of doing business rather than being socialized.

A new Democratic administration will restore the integrity of occupational and environmental inspection. The role of government is not to free corporations from profit-reducing regulations, responsibility for the health of employees and communities, and liability for environmental damage. The current Republican administration's priorities are reflected in their rolling back of thirty years of Clean Air standards and the routine demotion and firing of whistleblowers.

For example, this government has sought to exonerate the corporate giant Massey Energy, a major Republican contributor, of responsibility for the most serious environmental spill in the history of the eastern United States, a release of 300 million gallons of coal waste on October 11,

2000, from a 72-acre refuse impoundment near Inez, Kentucky. The polluted slurry flowed into two creeks, along 100 miles of riverbed leading to the Ohio River—a disaster twenty-five times the scope of the one caused by the *Exxon Valdez.*

An engineer who then headed the National Mine Health and Safety Academy (MSHA), Jack Spadero, reported that Massey intentionally misrepresented the depth of the coal barrier in its reservoir in reports to the government. Following an investigation during the last months of the Clinton government, the new Bush administration appointed Dave Lauriski, a former mining industry executive, as the new head of MSHA. The agency then quickly cut short the investigation, lowered the number of violations under consideration from eight to the two least serious, and repudiated and then retaliated against the previous investigators.

Said Spadero, "It appeared to me they thought we were getting too close to issuing serious violations to the mining company.... I have never seen anything so corrupt and lawless in my entire career, what I saw regarding interference with a federal investigation.... I've been in government since Richard Nixon. I've been through the Reagan administration, Carter, and Clinton. I've never seen anything like this."

Energy

A new national energy policy is crucial to the economy, the security, and the environmental health of our nation. Industry, individual citizens, and government all have roles to play in making energy efficiency the rule, not the exception. In addition to policies and practices that encourage conservation and efficiency, we must move from using predominantly "dirty" and limited fossil fuels to the widespread deployment of renewable and "clean" energy sources such as those based on water, the sun, and wind. No single solution will meet our society's energy needs, which must be satisfied instead by an array of technologies that do not deplete natural resources or destroy the ecosystems we depend on for life. In other words, energy solutions must be sustainable both environmentally and economically.

Our current energy system relies primarily on fossil fuels (coal, oil, and natural gas) and nuclear energy. The latter creates enormous risks, as exemplified by the Three Mile Island accident, since which the U.S. has built no new nuclear reactors, though about a hundred are still operating in this country.

Fossil fuels account for about 85 percent of current U.S. fuel consumption, with oil used mainly for our gasoline, not electricity generation. (Thus we do not need to drill for more oil domestically to ensure the stability of our electrical grid—a popular misconception.) Nonetheless, burning fossil fuels for electricity generation is the single greatest source of air pollution in the U.S. In addition to causing cancer and other chronic health problems, the burning of fossil fuels contributes to global warming because it is the major source of carbon dioxide emissions. Furthermore, it degrades valuable land and water resources by polluting the immediate environment as well as creating acid rain that can fall far from the generation site. Even the exploration and extraction of fossil fuels damages the environment through oil spills, strip mining, and the opening up and subsequent ruination of Earth's last remaining wilderness areas. Currently wars are fought to secure a share of the diminishing supply of oil, accentuating the fact that reducing America's reliance on oil is crucial to our immediate and long-term national security.

Under the coming Democratic administration, the United States will establish as a high priority the development and use of cost-effective alternative energy-generation technologies. Goals will include reducing imports of oil and reliance on petroleum and other limited resources, as well as diminishing the impacts of satisfying America's energy needs on public health and the global environment. Clean, renewable sources of energy release no carbon dioxide when used and produce no air pollutants when burned. Already approximately 6 percent of all the energy consumed in the U.S. comes from renewable sources; this small amount saves almost half a billion tons of CO_2 emissions per year.

Government policies are desperately needed to speed this conversion process. Measures to be adopted by the future administration will include:

- Government action to induce price adjustments favoring renewable fuels and technologies in industry and transportation and to eliminate barriers to their adoption.
- A steadily increasing requirement that by the year 2020, at least 20 percent of our electricity is generated through renewable sources.
- Tax incentives to bolster an increasing percentage of renewable electricity generation.
- Requirements that government purchasers of energy include renewable sources.
- Instituting a small tax on utility revenues to fund new renewable-energy development.
- Setting efficiency standards for buildings, vehicles (see "Transportation"), and appliances.
- Encouraging greater investment in public transportation.

- Honoring international treaties aimed at reducing carbon emissions and the threat of global warming.

Until the above measures are implemented, our economy is held hostage to outside factors, some of them political, some geological, all of them substantially out of American control. Immediate moves toward conservation and use of renewables will protect existing fossil fuel stocks and make us less dependent on military might and political upheaval. In the short run, the use of petroleum must be intelligent and careful so that industry has plenty of energy to fuel the economy, citizens have access to reliable electricity and gas for daily life, and we are not overly dependent on imports.

Transportation

Driving carries severe environmental impacts. Because 40 percent of the oil used by America fuels light trucks and cars, it is critical that we increase the gas mileage obtained by vehicles on U.S. roads. In furtherance of the goal of energy independence and reliance on renewable sources, the United States government will create incentives to motor vehicle fuel efficiency by broadening and increasing the penalties imposed on fuel-inefficient vehicles in the form of luxury and gasoline taxes, while increasing the tax benefits available to hybrid and alternative-energy vehicles. Fuel economy standards need to be increased to above 40 miles per gallon by 2012 and 55 mpg by 2020. The adoption of fuel-efficient technologies would save more oil by 2012 than is recoverable from the Arctic. Other studies show that an improvement of only 2.7 miles per gallon would eliminate our need for Persian Gulf oil. We simply cannot drill our way out of the current gasoline supply problems.

Already it is possible for automakers to produce passenger vehicles that achieve more than 40 mpg. Using hybrid technologies, the fuel economy level rises to 55 mpg. With emerging fuel cell technology, we approach 80 mpg. Better gas mileage reduces both global warming emissions and air pollution, while also contributing to a more stable economy and national security by reducing the dependence on oil imports and the uncertainty of rising gas prices.

The recent explosion of SUV and light truck sales has seriously eroded this nation's fuel efficiency and increased the reliance on foreign oil. It is long past time to close the absurd loophole in the thirty-year-old corporate average fuel economy, or CAFE, law that sets minimum fuel-economy standards. As currently formulated, this law exempts gas-guzzling SUVs from the standards that all other passenger cars must adhere to by including them in a category with farm vehicles. SUVs and light trucks account for approximately 50 percent of all new vehicles sold in the U.S. today, yet are subject to fuel-consumption requirements that are about 25 percent lower than those that apply to cars. They are also allowed to emit more pollution. Congressional Research Service reports show that increasing the fuel economy of light trucks and SUVs to match that of cars would save as much oil as would be produced by drilling in the Arctic National Wildlife Refuge. Only through federal fuel economy standards can we lock in gains throughout the auto industry. The Bush administration added insult to injury when it created an additional tax incentive (up to $100,000!) for people purchasing new trucks and work vehicles that exceed 6,000 pounds; this must be repealed immediately.

Tax credits are an important part of accelerating the emergence of advanced-technology vehicles. The new administration will develop and promote strategies to increase fuel efficiency for vehicles and reduce the adverse impacts of the U.S. transportation system. Measures will include:

- Immediately closing the SUV loophole and setting the higher CAFE standards for all vehicles on U.S. roads.
- Encouraging automakers to build and sell battery-electric, hybrid electric, and fuel-cell vehicles.

- Continuing to clean up conventional autos, public transit buses, school buses, and other diesel on- and off-road vehicles through better tailpipe technologies and other approaches. Diesel emissions are a major culprit in our deteriorating urban air quality, making a major contribution to childhood asthma and other growing health problems.
- Encouraging vehicle tax incentives, thereby ensuring that cars and trucks eligible for credits are substantially cleaner and more fuel-efficient than the average car.
- Investing in public transportation such as light rail systems, Amtrak, high-speed trains, aviation systems, and other choices besides driving.

Agriculture and Farm Policy

In the U.S. and abroad, the food supply is increasingly falling into the hands of a few large corporations, continuing the decline in the economics of small family farms and threatening food security (availability, accessibility, and use) in many parts of the world. And we are poised on the edge of a brave new world: The development of genetically modified organisms (GMOs) could change the very face of food production and crop genomes, as likely toward famines as windfall harvests. A new administration in the White House must address these trends in agriculture and their impact on traditional farming, biodiversity, and food security.

We believe the time has come for an entirely different approach to agriculture and trade, one that prioritizes food sovereignty and the preservation of rural livelihoods: the right of peoples, communities, and countries to define their own agricultural, labor, fishing, food, and land policies and to plant, harvest, and eat in ways which are ecologically, socially, economically, and culturally appropriate to their unique circumstances.

Furthermore, industrial agricultural practices such as the overuse of fertilizers and chemicals, overgrazing, the dumping of agricultural waste, and the runoff of pesticides into streams and groundwater severely damage air, water, and soil quality. "Free Trade" agreements continue to leave communities and taxpayers with public-health hazards and cleanup costs while corporations reap profits from industrial agriculture.

Global trade agreements related to agriculture are a large part of the problem the next administration must face. It is impossible for small farmers in any nation to compete with large-scale subsidized agribusiness. The demise of the American family farm is real and has been documented for decades, but in smaller, poorer countries, the consequences of global agribusiness have been even more disastrous if less visible. And as agribusiness gains an ever larger share, eliminating small producers and subsistence farmers, food security declines. The danger of the political control of food and the right to plant seeds—something that would have been considered laughable a generation ago—is now a gathering cloud.

The WTO's Agreement on Agriculture (AOA) aims to eliminate tariffs to promote free trade. But free trade in foodstuffs favors large farming and food-producing corporations, particularly those that are subsidized by the U.S. government. Many countries, including the U.S., maintain high tariffs to protect local industries. Because of the critical importance of food, governments should be allowed to set and control policies that encourage adequate and efficient food production, and to set tariffs to assist farmers in times of crisis in global market prices.

An ecological farming movement has been growing worldwide for more than thirty years. The new administration will evaluate future investments in agriculture with an eye to promoting organic and sustainable production systems and small farms. Agriculture policies for the next administration will include as priorities:

- farmland and watershed protection and restoration.
- the restoration of polycultural diversity and appropriate scaling to farming systems.

- supporting sustainable farming and economic and socially just farm labor practices while establishing disincentives for non-sustainable farming and business practices.
- eliminating the use of toxic insecticides, fungicides, and herbicides as rapidly as possible.

The patenting of seeds, plants, animals, and their components is another evolving aspect of international agriculture that threatens both food security and the democratic process. Trade agreements intended to provide global protection for trademarks, copyrights, and patents are now being over-extended to apply to life forms, which should be exempt from patenting. Because this agreement undermines access to and distribution of seeds and therefore impacts our food supply, the provisions of the treaty on Trade-Related Intellectual Property Rights (TRIPs) that permit multinationals to patent seeds originally developed in nature or by farmers must be abolished.

Current agreements under the WTO require that GMOs must be treated no differently from their conventional counterparts. We condemn this transparent attempt to place profit before human safety, which makes consumers into guinea pigs for the powerful biotech industry. In addition, it is credibly argued by scientists that the spread of GMOs will drastically reduce biodiversity by contaminating conventional crops through the spread of pollen. No satisfactory protections currently exist to safeguard the public food supply from known or unknown dangers of this new technology. Policies must be developed and put in place to require that GMOs be proven safe and controllable before they can be sold, used, or transported across borders.

Fisheries

While supporting the Sustainable Fisheries Act of 1996, we will close its loopholes by amendments and by developing additional legislation to end overfishing within the declared 200-mile exclusive economic zone of the United States and its possessions. We will set enforceable, stock-specific catch limits; establish enforceable by-catch and non-target species limits; protect and improve habitats for fishery resources; aggressively rebuild depleted fish populations; and update fishery infrastructure and information systems.

We advocate a mandatory recovery process for key overfished species, one that also provides protection for non-target species. While we are sensitive to the plight of individual fishers wanting to go back to sea during their working lifetimes, the depleted fish populations cannot be replenished through the application of loopholes or political pressure. If we want fish tomorrow, we must aggressively protect those fish today. If we want to deed a $50 billion industry to our children, if we want a living ocean in the coming decades, we must act now while there are still enough fish to restore populations. Federal management has already led to the partial recovery of the notoriously over-fished Atlantic swordfish and summer flounders, some species of mackerel off the southeastern coast, red snapper in the Gulf of Mexico, lobsters in the Gulf of Maine, and tanner and snow crabs in Alaskan waters. Restoring the Atlantic cod, a hallmark of the founding of our nation, is a priority of our administration.

Additionally, we propose the following strong measures:

- We will set aside marine protected spawning and nursery areas, no-take reserves where fish can grow both larger and more abundant. Fisheries recover at least twice as fast in reserves than in places where catches are merely limited. Fish from these reserves will also spill over into the general marine environment.
- We will oppose the Freedom to Fish Act, preferring a zoning plan that, by trading access in certain areas for putting other areas off-limits, serves both fishers and the restoration of stock.
- We propose legislation gradually phasing out harmful

fishing methods such as the popular dragging bottom-trawl and much rarer use of explosives that are particularly destructive to the ocean floor, as well as pair trawling and drift-netting. Purse-seining must be watched closely for its negative impacts. We will restrict harvesting on most coral reefs until recovery.

- We will initiate a "public awareness" campaign, encouraging consumers to participate in fisheries recovery by boycotting overfished and illegally fished species as well as fishing methods that yield unregulated by-catches of non-target species and undersized fish. Present boycotts and eco-labeling have helped slow the decline of Atlantic swordfish, Beluga caviar, and Chilean seabass, while also protecting dolphins from tuna nets. We will use the White House as a "bully pulpit" to promote ecologically harvested species.

III. PROGRESS

We do not believe that the problem with the U.S. federal government is that it is too big. It is a bureaucracy, and it is in the nature of all bureaucracies to become conservative, self-defensive, and self-perpetuating. These are tendencies we must constantly push against in the election of our representatives to the two houses of the Congress.

The problem with the federal government in 2004 is that it is being used to pursue a set of reactionary agendas. The Bush administration has seized on the 9/11 attacks as an excuse to dilute individual privacy and constrain freedom of speech, freedom of association, and the freedom to travel, all in the name of purported "security." It has used the economic slowdown of recent years as a pretense for making the federal system of taxation much more regressive. It is undermining the constitutional wall that separates the state from religion, and seeking through propaganda to confuse the common good with policies that benefit its friends who run large corporations. It is manipulating the legislative branch to gain leverage to shape the judicial branch.

The federal government ought to be used, as we noted above, to foster and reinforce equality and democracy in the United States and to provide those social and educational programs that are beyond the scope of the individual or of local government. What "reinvention" is required is to improve the government's effectiveness at serving the public's needs. Government should emphasize results over red tape, providing quality service, in partnership with the private sector where appropriate, to achieve common goals. We believe the Internet has the potential to be a liberating and democratic tool, and under Democratic leadership the growing e-government initiative will break down barriers to public services, reduce costs, and make government more accessible for all.

As a general principle, we seek ever-increasing professionalism in our government departments and agencies and in their leadership. Where possible, we urge that protection and responsibility be given to whistle-blowers, individuals who have demonstrated both a commitment to their agencies' goals and a determined professionalism.

Ethics

When it comes to governance, ethics is more than just a traditional standard of behavior. If those who direct our policies and represent us to the world are not ethical, then the society that elects and follows them becomes less ethical. If that society is the leading democracy and strongest military force on the planet, the entire world becomes less ethical.

At this complicated time in history, it is absolutely necessary that those in charge of our country embrace standards that the rest of society can admire and emulate. Yet the message of the Republican administration in 2004 is that it is permissible to lie and deceive, as long as it is for a good cause; it is permissible to misrepresent in order to advance your own self-interests; it is ethical to take from the poor and give to the rich as long as you can fabricate a passable explanation that such activity is really for the good of all; it is American to pollute wilderness, squander resources, and contaminate air and water as long as these events serve capital appreciation, greater profit, and the development of unfettered free markets; elective office is an opportunity not to serve the people but to feather the nests of one's supporters and lobbyists; and the spoils of victory supersede the responsibility of leadership.

The consequences of this behavior go far beyond any immediate impact of the actions. Despite shallow and pseudo-Christian moralizing, the Republican message to the citizenry of this country is that we might as well litter, bully, vandalize, drive gas-guzzling cars, cheat on taxes, deceive one another in business, make merchandise that falls apart, advertise falsely, produce and franchise unhealthy foods and drinks, sell video games featuring murder and mutilation (and even police assassination) to kids, ignore the plight of the poor, the jobless, and the homeless, hoard property and money, take advantage of immigrants, commit unspeakable crimes out of imagined lusts and envies, seek revenge for minor slights, and, in general, behave as selfishly as the compromised law allows us to get away with. Such people worship a strangely selective God who allows mind-boggling greed and cruelty in public life, encourages profligacy, yet punishes some sex between some consenting adults and all uses of recreational drugs (but not alcohol). Either they don't care about future generations or are leaving them, as Ronald Reagan's Secretary of the Interior James Watt recommended, to the Second Coming and the Rapture.

This is the vision of the United States introduced by the Republican Party of the 1980s and now in full ascendancy. A society based on these principles will not long survive. It is a society, ultimately, of white-collar criminals, gangs, serial killers, kids with assault weapons, road ragers, overweight couch potatoes, scofflaws, weapons in space, paramilitaries at home and throughout the developing world, and skyrocketing deficits. It is a society obsessed with glitter, glamour, fame, vicarious reality, junk food, lotteries, and commercialized sex, but hollow at its core. It is a society ill-prepared to challenge disciplined and hostile fanatics from madrasas, even in the realm of patriotism, morals, and ideas. It is a society doomed to anarchy.

The Republicans tell us that the world outside our country, the world from which they are protecting us, is a scary world. It is a place where women, children, drugs, and nuclear weapons are sold in back alleys and corporate boardrooms, where international crime rings dominate whole industries, a world soon to be controlled by terrorists and mobs. What they do not tell us is that this is the world they are actively creating—a world that terrifies its inhabitants, thereby ensuring their own political longevity and increasing power. They are not interested in protecting the people; they are interested in the power that comes from leading a frightened citizenry.

Leadership

Leadership means many things. It means acting in exemplary ways, offering and acting on a vision, and providing a role model. In the context of the United States in these tumultuous years of the early 21st century, however, it means above all else standing tall in the face of crisis and making good and courageous decisions.

We do not have such a leader. We have instead a president who in the face of the 9/11 attacks on our country fled on Air Force One to a secret location—not for safety, but because the president was not capable of offering leadership, and his handlers wanted him out of the public eye until his speech could be written, his actions programmed. This will not do. We need a leader who, when unexpectedly coming under enemy fire, acts decisively, selflessly, and courageously.

The Republicans would have us believe that we have a leader who stands up to America's enemies and will protect us in the face of unprecedented threats. The Republicans would have us believe that we have a courageous leader who puts the safety of our people first.

This is demonstrably not true. Thanks to the Supreme Court, we have as our president a man who avoided wartime military service in his youth. And it is not only the president; George W. Bush has surrounded himself with others who also avoided service. These are the very men and women who turn away from the prospect of championing peace, choosing instead to challenge and goad our enemies to attack us. They belittle the grievances of the downtrodden of the Earth, inciting them to join our enemies and swell their ranks for generations to come. Gun-toting wannabe cowboys, they have no imagination for solutions beyond war. They valorize war not because they are good at it, wise in the use of it, or even understand it and its real complexities and ramifications, but because their diplomatic repertoire contains little else.

They act in this manner because they rightly perceive themselves as threatened. They act on behalf of the wealthiest of the wealthy; they represent those who hoard far beyond their needs and thus rightfully feel threatened by the have-nots of this nation and the world.

We have a leadership that does not value the arts, does not support basic scientific research, marginalizes philanthropy, and sees no reason not to turn its political victories into further spoils for those who need them least. We have a leadership that asks not what we can do for the country but what the country can do for them: How much can we take from the public coffers to reward our backers? How much can we steal without causing a revolt? How much can we lie without being found out? For how long can we divert attention from our epic deeds of corporate theft and favoritism for the wealthy?

We of the Democratic Party offer leadership and service. We offer protection *and* reconciliation with the larger world. We offer a future that is something more than an embattled aging empire preparing for an apocalyptic fight with barbarians and terrorists.

Our party failed at leadership when it offered a president who was morally flawed, who heedlessly and hedonistically put his own appetites ahead of his responsibility to the nation. Mr. Clinton's behavior was unconscionable. However, reprehensible though he may have been in his personal life, he was also a president who worked hard to serve those who needed it most. In his place we now have a representative of the wealthiest and least charitable polities in the United States, a man whose interests are not ours and whose policies and actions threaten the very existence of this country.

Campaign Finance Reform

The power of money has corrupted our system of elections. Money comes from those who can afford to give it, and typically these are individuals and companies with interests that can be served by government decisions.

Ironically, much of the need for money with which to conduct campaigns is driven by the costs of buying TV time, a necessity in national campaigns as well as those being conducted in large states. Yet the airwaves belong to us; the Communications Act of 1934 established the Federal Communications Commission and directed it to license broadcasting stations using as its standard "the public convenience, interest, or necessity."

We believe that representative democracy and the electoral process in the U.S. will best be served by strengthening the system of public financing of elections and at the same time requiring of all FCC licensees that they make specified amounts of time available at no charge, and in accordance with newly promulgated FCC regulations, to bona fide candidates for public office.

Enforcing the will of the people as expressed in the voting booth is best served by insisting as well on election by a majority vote, using the increasingly popular Instant Runoff Voting (IRV) system. Instant runoff voting accommodates multiple candidates in single-seat races and ensures that a "spoiler" effect will not result in undemocratic outcomes. Instant runoff voting involves each voter ranking candidates in order of preference. This allows voters to vote for their favorite candidate without fear of helping elect their least favorite candidate, and it ensures that the winner enjoys true support from a majority of the voters. Plurality voting, used in most U.S. elections, does not meet these basic requirements for a fair election system that promotes wide participation. IRV, on the other hand, promotes positive, issue-based campaigns because candidates will seek second- and third-choice votes, and it creates a clearer mandate for a winning candidate's agenda, giving better direction for policy-making.

The Separation of Church and State

Pronouncements from the White House and Capitol Hill notwithstanding, the United States is not a Christian nation. While Christians may outnumber Americans of any other religious persuasion, this is a secular nation. Any president or administration official who claims otherwise is wrong.

Charity, tolerance, and compassion are spiritual and ethical virtues that transcend particular churches. They also ought to be virtues embraced by all those who seek to represent us as public officials. But belief systems that set one group above another in the eyes of God and that prophesy doom as punishment for the sins of not believing or for violating sectarian precepts have no place in politics. They are exactly what our forefathers intended to escape when they set up a new nation and wrote new laws separating it from all existing churches.

The U.S. Constitution is a wholly secular document. It contains no mention of Christianity or Jesus Christ. In fact, the Constitution refers to religion only twice—in the First Amendment, which bars laws "respecting an establishment of religion or prohibiting the free exercise thereof," and in Article VI, which prohibits "religious tests" for public office. The principle of church-state separation is essential to protect America's religious freedom. Individual rights and diversity cannot be maintained if the government promotes Christianity or if our government takes on the trappings of a faith-based state.

It is troubling that so many in our country now feel that advancing political positions and seeking political power in the name of their God is not only acceptable but divinely warranted. Such zeal has in the past led to discrimination and the legislation of morality. Beliefs driven by competing views of divine imperatives can never compromise or be welded into a democratic consensus. The separation of church and state must be absolute and inviolable.

The National Bioethics Advisory Committee (NBAC), created by the Bush administration, replicates a similar advisory panel from the Clinton years, consisting of recognized scholars from the realms of science, philosophy, law, and religion. Our administration will appoint an equivalent panel, but we will not impose political restraints on their views or otherwise tamper with their reports or muzzle them. Members of the Bush panel have been replaced by notoriously conservative alternate members for solely ideological and political reasons. This stacking of the committee in favor of President Bush's personal and political preferences on various bioethical issues is a national embarrassment. Large portions of the scientific community have signed a petition expressing a vote of no-confidence in NBAC, given its biased nature. Academics, research, and science must not be tainted by politics and religion.

We will let ethicists within science tackle thorny decisions about stem cells and other biological and medical issues. Whether stem cells can be harvested ethically, whether their conversion into therapies will ease suffering and cure disease effectively enough to justify the invasive technologies for producing them—these are issues that ought not to be decided on the basis of religious beliefs. In a secular society, they are decisions to be made for medical and social reasons. To do otherwise, imposing taboos on some research in order to appease religious groups or win votes, is to trade medicine for superstition, and also to turn over to the rest of the world the opportunity to develop the most promising new technologies.

Internationally, religious hegemonies confronting each other with weapons of mass destruction threaten life on the planet. The United States must not be drawn into such holy wars. We will conduct our nation's dealings with the rest of the world with fairness, morality, and human dignity, informed by and expressing the best of the Judeo-Christian as well as other spiritual traditions, including native American ones. But we will not wage holy wars or crusades. Instead, the United States must work to create a world community in which priests and ayatollahs can coexist but do not command legions. Furthermore, we will make it clear to the rest of the world that we stand for equal opportunity for all faiths and will not tolerate the biblicization of our government's policies, foreign or domestic.

While it will be uncomfortable to some, consistent support for this position requires that we remove the words "under God" from the Pledge of Allegiance and the words "in God we trust" from our currency.

Education

As the United States transitions from the Industrial Age to the global Information Age, the way we educate our citizens must change as well. Everyone, young and old, must have access to the knowledge and skills to participate in the evolving economy.

If current policies continue, however, the divide between those who have access to services and resources and those who do not will continue to grow. Lack of literacy is a community development issue, affecting health, housing, well-being, and most other aspects of living. As a nation we therefore must invest more, rather than less, in education, lifelong learning, skills development, and research and development.

It is hardly radical to demand that every child be provided the highest-quality education, that every high school graduate master the basics of reading and math. But given the direction of the Bush administration's education policy, this is neither what we have nor the direction in which we are going (though with a kind of Orwellian logic, they have labeled their imperative "No Child Left Behind"). We urge the restoration of and increase in support for preschool programs that engender higher reading and achievement levels, higher graduation rates, and greater success in the workplace. We must invest in our crumbling school infrastructure and reverse the budget-induced classroom crowding.

Of paramount importance, we must support our teachers adequately. Teachers are no less important to the health and success of our children than medical professionals and must be held to similarly high standards and paid commensurately. Teachers should live in the neighborhoods where they teach, and effective programs must be developed to allow them to buy homes. Leadership in these policy and budget directions must come from the White House.

We oppose language-based discrimination in all its forms. We encourage so-called English-plus initiatives, believing that multilingualism is increasingly valuable in the global economy.

We believe that taxes paid by the public should go to support public education. While school choice is every parent's right, we oppose and call on the administration and Congress to bar private-school vouchers that drain resources from public schools.

"No Child Left Behind," the Bush administration's Procrustean rewrite of the Elementary and Secondary Education Act, must be rewritten. NCLB is a fundamentally punitive law that uses flawed standardized tests to label schools as failures and punish them with counterproductive sanctions. It must be transformed into a supportive law that truly promotes school improvement and makes good on the promise to leave no child behind.

The law does contain some positive elements. It authorizes the federal government to increase funding for the education of low-income students. It mandates that states eliminate the academic "achievement gap" that exists between different groups of students, particularly those who historically have not been well served. It also requires states, districts, and schools to find ways to educate all students successfully.

Unfortunately, NCLB does not authorize nearly enough funding to meet its new requirements, making the requirement to eliminate all test-score gaps in twelve years an unfunded state mandate. The Bush administration sought almost no increase in expenditures for the act for this fiscal year. Meanwhile, states are suffering their worst budget crises since World War II, and as a result they are cutting education as well as the social programs needed by low-income people.

In addition, there is broad agreement that the NCLB assessment requirements and the accountability provisions attached to them are rigid, harmful, and ultimately unworkable. They are forcing harmful curricula changes, further devaluing non-tested subjects like social studies, music, and art. In effect, they are transforming our schools into test-preparation programs. Ironically, this new educational regimen, championed by a political party that supposedly stands for individual rights and dignity, punishes the teachers who choose to work in the nation's most under-resourced schools.

The first step toward improving schools, according to NCLB, is to allow parents to transfer their children to a school with higher test scores. But the law does not guarantee that classroom seats will be available. We believe these provisions are intended to manufacture a demand for school alternatives and ultimately to transfer funds and students to profit-making private school corporations through vouchers. Such marketplace solutions to the difficult and complex problems of schooling will not improve the public school system; they are more likely to lead to its dismantling.

Congress must overhaul this law, and it must fund the new version adequately. We must insist that the federal government ensure that equitable funding is available to all students, and support the states in making that possible. Congress should cut back on mandatory testing, prohibit the use of high-stakes testing for graduation or grade promotion, and encourage schools to use multiple forms of assessment.

A college education is no longer merely a desirable middle-class option; it is a necessity. Participants in today's—and even more pointedly, tomorrow's—economy must have the opportunity to continue learning and upgrading their skills. The states' public college systems are commendable steps in the direction of universal higher education, but they are suffering badly in the face of the draconian Bush administration funding cutbacks. It must be enacted as U.S. policy that every citizen has a right to a college education, and that mandate must be funded adequately.

Health Care

Books have been written on the illness that has befallen the U.S. health-care system. We feel no need to repeat that work. It is by now self-evident that what was once a pluralistic health care system has, for all but the most wealthy, become a system run by corporate oligopolies that excludes rather than includes. People today are waiting longer for medical appointments. Fewer people are getting a doctor of their choice. Medical-care options are eroding almost by the week, even more rapidly outside our big cities. We look forward to the exploration of the possible future shape of a broader, gentler, more patient-oriented health system.

The health plans proposed during both the Clinton and Bush administrations are not health plans but money plans. They propose legislatively to adjust relative balances within a marketplace of HMOs, insurance companies, drug companies, lawyers, and businesses. None of them propose any significant change in health care itself. Medical care today is almost entirely about insurance, not health. Physicians are being given monetary incentives to deny care. Their diagnostic and treatment options are tainted by financial considerations. Pre-existing illnesses are being used to deny coverage.

That means no change in a situation in which most patients are given little guidance in how to care for themselves, prevent disease, or aid in their own cure. Instead, outdated metaphors from the age of manufacturing abound: We are encouraged to view doctors as all-knowing mechanics and our bodies as machines about which we are ignorant. Processed rapidly as though on an assembly line, we are urged to rely on outside experts to fine-tune our bodies, to give them healthy lives. Health and life itself have become commodities controlled by corporations.

Given the skyrocketing cost of medical care and treatment, for an astonishingly large portion of the U.S. population major life decisions are being shaped by health-insurance issues: Where shall we live? What career shall I pursue? Can I take some time off work? Can I retire? All of which translates into, can I get or keep my health insurance? According to the American Public Health Association, "The lack of health care coverage is detrimental to the individuals, their families, and the community at large. Due to the high costs of health care, uninsured individuals and their families have difficulties getting quality health care when they are sick. They tend to delay treatments until their illnesses become serious and are less likely to seek routine preventive health services that can avert or detect major illnesses early on. As a result, they are usually sicker and more likely to die sooner than people with health insurance.

"The lack of health insurance aggravates the financial burden of the whole community. Since the uninsured tend to delay necessary treatment, they are often sicker and therefore more expensive to treat when they finally seek care. Also, when they decide to seek care, they frequently turn to the nearest hospital emergency room, which is an expensive and inefficient way to get care. Furthermore, the primary providers of care to the uninsured, such as public hospitals, teaching hospitals, academic health centers, and non-profit community hospitals, incur heavy losses from high rates of uncompensated care. In turn, these providers are forced to cut back on their services to all patients or even close their facilities."

Even within the managed health-care system, insufficient connection is made between diet and lifestyle and health. Compare the resources and investments in invasive reactive procedures with current expenditures on education and preventative care. People are not taught health, but instead are treated for diseases. Although medical professionals are on the front lines, these diseases are diagnosed and then addressed according to protocols established as much, if not more, by insurers and pharmaceutical corporations, entities with an investment in what products and treatments are used.

Why are we faced with this crisis? It's because we perpetuate a "health care" system that produces profit by denying care, while over-pricing what is available. Three or four hospital chains and managed care plans own or control a growing share of medical practice. Success in the new medical marketplace is determined by financial clout, not medical quality. In their pursuit of financial return, HMOs are racing to take over Medicare, despite evidence that HMOs have actually increased Medicare costs. And in addition to the obscene profits pharmaceutical vendors are realizing from the domestic sales of their products, the large drug firms appear to be preparing to directly take over much of specialty medical care. Merck, Lilly, and others are developing "Disease Management" subsidiaries to subcontract with HMOs to care for patients with expensive chronic diseases such as depression, diabetes, asthma, and cancer.

According to Physicians for a National Health Program, private insurers take, on average, 13 percent of premium dollars for overhead and profit. In big managed care plans, the figure is even higher, approximating 30 percent. For comparison, overhead consumes less than 2 percent of funds in the fee-for-service Medicare program and less than 1 percent in Canada's program.

Physicians in the U.S. must process patients quickly and formulaically. Hence, the emphasis is on cost saving, margin of profitability, and standardization rather than treatment. They face massive bureaucratic costs that they must pass along to patients or patient insurers, perpetuating the upward spiral. The average office-based U.S. doctor employs 1.5 clerical and managerial staff, spends 44 percent of gross income on overhead, and devotes 134 hours of his/her own time annually to billing. Canadian physicians employ 0.7 clerical/administrative staff, spend 34 percent of their gross income for overhead, and trivial amounts of time on billing.

According to the General Accounting Office, administrative savings from a shift to a single-payer system would total about 10 percent of overall health spending. These administrative savings, about $100 billion annually, would be enough to cover all of the uninsured as well as to virtually eliminate co-payments, deductibles, and exclusions for those who now have inadequate plans—all without any increase in total health spending.

Because of the costliness and profitability-oriented restrictiveness of the system, more than 45 million Americans have no medical insurance, and millions more are struggling to maintain their coverage in the face of rising premiums, deductibles, and co-payments.

Private insurance companies must be removed as the shapers of the health care equation, and the resources they convert to profit must be redirected to paying for care. A single-payer system simply is better for patients and better for doctors, and a newly elected Democratic president must make this transition a top priority.

We propose also to nurture and develop alternatives to conventional medicine and to begin the process of meaningfully researching the benefits of competing systems so that useful and effective techniques can be separated from quackery. Among the systems that can contribute to care, with more emphasis on the specific needs of patients and long-term health management and prevention—and at a much lower cost—are osteopathy, naturopathy, traditional Chinese medicine, and Ayurvedic (traditional Indian) medicine. Inevitably, this undertaking will lead to a reexamination of the monopoly on healing granted to the American Medical Association and the pharmaceutical companies with which it is allied—a monopoly supported by both political parties. The result of this monopolization has been a very expensive, over-technologized, unresponsive system reflecting corporate rather than scientific or healing values.

The Mentally Ill

There are three times as many men and women with mental illness in U.S. prisons as in mental health hospitals. According to Human Rights Watch, one in six U.S. prisoners (350,000) is mentally ill. Many of them suffer from serious illnesses such as schizophrenia, bipolar disorder, or major depression.

The high rate of incarceration of the mentally ill is a consequence of underfunded, disorganized, and fragmented community mental health services. State and local governments have shut down mental health hospitals across the United States but failed to provide adequate alternatives. Many people with mental illness—particularly those who are poor, homeless, or struggling with substance-abuse problems—cannot get mental health treatment. Incapable of getting a job or fending for themselves, they are often forced to live on the street—a scandal for a society with our levels of wealth. If they commit a crime, even a low-level nonviolent offense, punitive sentencing laws mandate imprisonment.

If this is indeed a government *for* the people, the administration should set as a priority the development of a well-funded, coordinated, and comprehensive community mental health service network. Rather than re-opening mental health hospitals, we should use our tax dollars to invest in targeted programs situated in the communities of need. We must, and will, treat metal-illness sufferers in their own communities rather than in prison and as a public-health rather than a criminal-justice problem.

Housing

Decent housing is a fundamental human right and should be the birthright of every American. Housing must serve a continuum of populations. The needs for decent, affordable housing encompass emergency housing and supportive services for the homeless and for battered women, transitional housing for individuals and families beginning to take control over their lives, and permanent rental or homeownership housing.

The free market is not about affordable housing as a right. In no urban jurisdiction in the U.S. can a full-time minimum-wage worker afford the fair-market rent. On average, families across the country must earn $14.66 an hour—more than twice the minimum wage—to afford a two-bedroom apartment at fair-market rent.

More housing must be created, neighborhoods must be preserved or rebuilt with the involvement of those who live there, and the link between availability and profitability must be broken, because that link seals a barricade that bars low-income Americans from decent places to live.

An important step in addressing the housing availability and affordability crisis is the passage of the National Housing Trust Fund Act, which over the next decade would create 1.5 million new housing units that would be affordable by low-income renters and owners, using the profits generated by the Federal Housing Administration and other federal housing agencies as well as state matching funds.

These funds would be used for the production of new housing, preservation of existing federally assisted housing, and rehabilitation of existing private-market affordable housing. New housing units would be primarily rental units, and the focus would be on low-income households in mixed-income neighborhoods.

Despite the fact that the work of the Department of Housing and Urban Development (HUD) has been essential in promoting affordable housing and community development, Congress has cut HUD's budget by almost two-thirds over the last twenty-five years, and has been particularly ruthless at removing funding for existing Section 8 vouchers, which provide a lifeline for low-income families at risk for homelessness.

The new administration will seek to return HUD funding to pre-Reagan levels, to guarantee the continued full funding of existing Section 8 vouchers, and to support funding of new incremental vouchers. Funds also must be restored to the Agriculture Department's Section 515 Rural Rental Housing program, and passage secured for the Rural Rental Housing Assistance Act, which would create a new $250 million fund to acquire, rehabilitate, or construct rural rental housing for low-income people, with priority for very low-income households.

Prison Reform

The U.S. leads the rest of the world in the use of prison as a solution for social problems. From 1980 to 2002, the number of people incarcerated in the nation's prisons, jails, juvenile facilities and detention centers quadrupled, from roughly 500,000 to 2.1 million people. With 6.6 million people in prison or jail or on probation and parole, the U.S. now has the largest penal system in the world.

The prison system influences the social, economic, and political life of all regions and sectors in the country. In addition to those incarcerated, 2.2 million people are employed in policing, corrections, and courts—substantially more than the 1.7 million Americans employed in higher education and the 600,000 employed in public welfare. Almost 7 percent of the adult population currently is behind bars on a felony conviction or living with a felony conviction record.

America's choice to use prison rather than other approaches to dealing with social problems has been an expensive one. From 1977 to 1999, total state and local expenditures on corrections rose by 946 percent—2.5 times the rate of increase of spending on all levels of education, and double the average increase for all state and local functions.

At a time when virtually every state in the country is grappling with the worst fiscal crisis since World War II, $1 in $14 spent by states is spent on corrections. In other words, the costs of maintaining the prison system are devastating state budgets, while the experience of prison is maiming millions of people every year.

Former prisoners often are punished for life. Depending on the state or jurisdiction, ex-prisoners and people once convicted of a felony can be barred from receiving public assistance or living in public housing. They may not be offered financial aid for college and, in many states, are prohibited from working in a wide array of public-sector jobs. This harms not only the ex-prisoner's chance of living a crime-free and productive life, but also families and communities by diminishing the chances that such citizens can become workers, caregivers, partners, and parents. Forty-eight of the fifty states bar prisoners and former prisoners from voting, and with 4 million people disenfranchised due to their involvement in the penal system, prisons now play a significant role in distorting American democracy and electoral outcomes.

Prison offers an object lesson in structural racism. While African Americans and Latinos are 25 percent of the national population and engage in criminal behavior at rates comparable to whites, they represent 63 percent of the people incarcerated in the U.S. According to current projections, nearly one in three African American men and one in six Latino men born in 2001 will go to prison at some time during their life, compared to one in seventeen white men. Half of all African American male high school dropouts are expected to serve time in prison by their early 30s, but only one in eight white male dropouts. Nearly twice as many black men in their early 30s have been in prison as have obtained a bachelor's degree.

Spending billions to incarcerate millions might make sense if it were keeping our communities safe. But research has shown that:

- 79 to 96 percent of the drop in violent crime seen recently cannot be explained by prison expansion.
- There is no relationship between use of prisons for drug offenses and lower drug use.

- Incarceration may drive up crime rates in places where a "tipping point" of more than 1 to 1.5 percent of a community is incarcerated.

Other research has shown that drug treatment is seven times more cost-effective than incarceration for dealing with drug use, and variety of other studies have shown that spending on crime prevention programs is a far more effective way of curbing crime in the future.

The American justice system once permitted judges to weigh all the facts of a case when determining a person's sentence. But in the 1970s and 1980s, the Congress and many state legislatures passed laws that force judges to give fixed prison terms to those convicted of specific crimes, most often drug offenses. Lawmakers believed that these harsh, inflexible sentencing laws would catch those at the top of the drug trade and deter others from entering it. In fact, though, mandatory minimum sentences increase the likelihood that low-level offenders will serve prison time by reducing the discretion of judges in determining the length of a sentence and their ability to place defendants on probation.

We need to work to restore balance to the sentencing system by ending the use of mandatory minimum sentencing laws and returning sentencing discretion to judges. In the longer term, we support the creation and use of sentencing commissions—arm's-length bodies that can report to legislatures on the impact of sentencing laws and suggest reforms to promote both effectiveness and fairness in the delivery of justice.

These and other policy steps must be designed to promote sentencing law changes that embrace the values of public safety, fairness, and the use of prison as a last-resort option. "Three Strikes" and "zero tolerance" laws may have catchy titles, but they often dole out devastatingly long sentences for minor offenses that do not serve any public safety goal and destroy the individual, their family, and communities.

Felony disenfranchisement, as unfair as it is, is only one of the more visible manifestations of the much larger problem of the collateral consequences of incarceration. Legal barriers to ex-prisoners' ability to get jobs, housing, social services, and food stamps constitute lifetime punishments that do more to punish the entire community than to serve any rehabilitative goal. We must re-embrace a just vision of rehabilitation that, at the very least, holds that once a sentence is complete and society's punitive price has been paid, all barriers to an ex-prisoner's safe return to his or her family, job, and community should be removed. Bans on people with felonies from working in certain sectors, occupying affordable housing, or receiving social service assistance must be removed and replaced with adequate educational, vocational, housing, and treatment services. For those leaving prison, we must shore up the parole services and community systems to support formerly incarcerated people in their goals of working, being parents, and living crime-free lives.

No country in the world imprisons as much of its population or is in the process of massive prison construction. This is nothing to be proud of. It reflects a simplistic solution to a series of complex problems, equivalent to our oversimplification of the War on Terrorism and with parallel results. We are breeding the elements and attitudes that we seek to eliminate, and we are hardening our criminals and making them more unforgiving and more resourceful. To mitigate the nation's prison dilemma, the government must end the "war on drugs," treat drug abuse and mental health as public health problems, end the use of mandatory minimums and "reform" sentencing laws, restore the right to vote for formerly incarcerated prisoners, and work to remove all barriers to their return to a productive life.

Public Support for the Arts

Currently the United States gives less public support to the arts than any other industrial democracy. Arguments against public subsidy typically invoke the risk of bureaucratic or ideologically motivated culture commissars who will interfere with the freedom of the artist and dictate what he or she should create. In fact, though, subsidized artists in Europe are handed money and allowed to do whatever they like.

We pledge to increase funding for the National Endowment for the Arts. We believe in the system of peer-panel review of applications. All funding procedures are imperfect, all are vulnerable to cronyism, but this is the least imperfect because working artists are ultimately better judges of the worth of an art project than any political appointees.

We pledge to resist all demagogic attacks on public support for the arts.

DC Statehood

Tremendous progress has been made in granting the franchise to virtually all disenfranchised groups living in the United States—save two. We've already addressed the issue of felons who have paid the court-mandated price for their crimes. The more than 600,000 people who live in our nation's capital have committed no crimes. They pay federal taxes, yet have no voting representation.

Surely there can be no greater irony than to have the seat

of the federal government be a colony and a living illustration of the "taxation without representation" issue first raised by James Otis in 1764. The new administration will work with Congress to pass the No Taxation Without Representation Act, introduced into the 108th Congress as S. 617.

Space Exploration

While space may still be the final frontier, we do not believe that going to Mars, as Mr. Bush has proposed, should be a high priority of the next administration. Refining the technologies and constructing the hardware to transport humans to our neighboring planet and bring them back while keeping them alive along the way and on the Martian surface—providing them with food, water, and air, and shielding them from charged particles from the sun—would cost anywhere from $800 billion to $1 trillion as compared to a modest $820 million recently spent to land two effective robots on the Martian surface. Most of this money would also have to be budgeted after the next presidency.

What humans would do on Mars that *Spirit* and *Opportunity* cannot (other than plant a flag, provide some photo ops, and hit a few golf balls) is of questionable value, hardly worth the ludicrous expenditure. The Bush administration speaks vaguely and ominously of "advancing U.S. scientific, security, and economic interests through a robust (manned) space-exploration program." We fear that "Mars" is a Republican subterfuge for the militarization of space. The chance of humans reaching Mars without catastrophe, conducting meaningful research there, setting up a useful base, and returning safely to Earth is extremely small. The likelihood of a series of such functional missions building on the results of one another is infinitesimal. It is unclear how attempting what would essentially be a premature symbolic landing on Mars would serve either the space program or the American people.

NASA's role in the manned exploration of space should emphasize projects that address the energy crisis on Earth. If there are, to quote a NASA homily, "no bucks without Buck Rogers," then a lunar base is a far more practical site for manned missions. The Moon is a potential source for new energy technologies that should at least be explored experimentally during the next administration, as we must begin to prepare for the inevitable decline of the Earth's oil reserves as well as address the residual problem of greenhouse-gas build-up. Potentially useful technologies include the mining of helium-3 light isotopes, deposited by billions of years of lunar exposure to the solar wind, for use in fusion reactors to generate thermonuclear power, should such technology turn out to be viable and safe. NASA could also explore the feasibility of beaming solar energy collected on the Moon to the Earth. This represents a possible cornucopia of sustainable energy for future civilizations.

We must be discerning in allocating funding in this area. While not being misled into "pork barrel" agendas by myopic and careerist scientists, we should continue to fund NASA's exploration of the other worlds in our solar system, especially Mars and the Jovian system, two places where we may find life. This is an endeavor that has the potential to increase humankind's comprehension of itself, promote the development of new technologies here on Earth, and expand our perspective on the nature of the universe.

The Hubble telescope and international space station should continue to be maintained. They represent the quest for knowledge and, even beyond their practical value, are icons for humanity engaging the vastness of the universe in a collectivity transcending culture and nation. The Hubble has contributed enormously to our understanding of cosmology, and some of this science may yet be of practical and economic value as we look to developing radically new digital technologies, nanotechnologies, and subatomic industries in the future. Not to continue this inquiry is to break our faith with both past and yet-to-be-born generations.

Conversely, to militarize space doesn't just militarize

space for the good guys. It means that anyone who can acquire the tools can use space as their battlefield—a year from now, a decade from now, or a generation from now.

To shut down an orbiting telescope and close a promising window on the unknown universe and its riddles for lack of administrative courage and funds while advocating orbiting weapons and the militarization of space sends the wrong message to the world.

We dismiss the safety issues regarding servicing the Hubble as a convenient red herring when compared to the much greater safety issues within the manned-space program at large. Additionally, it will cost at least $300 million to safely drop the Hubble into an ocean.

Government Openness

The existing Freedom of Information Act functions to protect government secrecy, which is antithetical to democratic governance. Current declassified documents are full of blacked-out sections, the results of public officials shielding themselves from legitimate scrutiny. The default assumption when it comes to information and documents held by federal, state, and local governments ought to be that they are accessible to the public unless there are extremely compelling reasons not to release them.

We propose revising the current rules to require that after a reasonable period of time, on the order of ten to twenty years, the entirety of all documents should be declassified. There is no reason why we shouldn't know the names of all the groups that the CIA funded in Chile during the 1973 campaign to overthrow Salvador Allende, or what specific policy directives President Richard Nixon gave to Henry Kissinger.

The typical counter-argument is that to reveal everything, even after time has passed, will seriously compromise our ability to work with intelligence assets in the future. That argument must be trumped by another: Not to reveal everything is to deny ourselves the public oversight without which democracy cannot function. Not to reveal everything would be to yield to high government officials the ability to cover up any action they choose—that is to say, to be unaccountable.

Democracy always poses a risk. But it should never be traded for the myth of total security.

In addition, if there are any classified documents about UFOs or extraterrestrials, this administration will declassify them.

Youth Corps

We propose the creation of a youth corps to begin to address simultaneously many of the problems we in the United States currently face and the danger that many of our young people are becoming disaffected and lost to productive society.

It is important to match the energies and perspectives of youth with problems that they are interested in helping to solve and are equipped to address. The youth corps would be a form of service for high-school dropouts and also college graduates not ready to start a career. Among the challenges that the Youth Corps could deal with are:

- Searching out ways to reduce our over-reliance on petroleum products. These could include observing patterns of everyday living to develop better ways to track automobile maintenance, new bicycle routes, and approaches to car-pooling and shared automobile use.

- Developing a more reliable and diversified agricultural base and food supply. This could include urban rooftop and neighborhood gardens, preparation of food boxes and delivery for the needy and homeless, setting up rural food stands, and teaching farmhands and migrant workers about the healthy growing of food.

- The need for alternative health practitioners. The program could provide training in manual medicine, herbs, and visualization techniques to young people, allowing them to relieve some of the medical burden in poor regions.

- Finding ways to reduce ecological destruction and pollution. The focus would be on finding and testing new methods of recycling, collecting litter, and reclaiming compromised land and bodies of water.

- Helping the homeless find shelter and food; identifying those among them that need medical or psychological treatment and arranging for them to get it; keeping them company and listening to their stories; and making a record of a lost sector of America.

- Mentoring and tutoring young people, helping with English as a second language, helping students find summer jobs.

- Visiting the forgotten elderly in institutions, providing company and recreation for them, listening to their stories, and helping to comfort those with Alzheimer's and other forms of senile dementia who are often isolated and mistreated by other residents.

In general, education should be practical and field-based as well as classroom-oriented. The Peace Corps made sense for an earlier generation. A new Youth Corps is needed to address a very different world, and a much more alienated and at-risk generation at home.

Personal Freedom

There is no better preparation for this presidential election campaign than to reread the Bill of Rights and the other amendments to the Constitution and contemplate how many of those constitutionally guaranteed freedoms the current administration has abrogated or weakened.

Since the separation of church and state must be maintained, marriage as licensed by any political unit of the United States can involve only a civil contractual relationship. It is not the business of government to make judgments about appropriateness when it comes to human relationships that do not harm others. We do not feel the need to involve ourselves in semantic quibbling over the name of the relationship between two consenting adults who choose to enter into a committed relationship. Whatever their genders and sexual preferences, they are entitled to the legal rights (and subject to the obligations) derived from marriage. If some want a religious marriage as well, they are free to obtain one without involving those outside their churches. But faith should not be used to deny others their rights to the same privileges and protections under law.

A women's right to choose is among the constitutional rights under assault by this administration. The right to equality and personal freedom, including the right to control one's own body, cannot be taken away. Any governmental attempt to do so is doomed to failure. The next Democratic administration will restate this obvious fact, and through policy, legislation, and judicial appointments chisel it into the fabric of American life for all time to come.

CONCLUSION

We recognize the irony of espousing progressive positions in a four-year electoral platform when many of these positions will run counter to the perceived self-interest of voters and will argue for wealth redistribution or renunciation. After all, political campaigns are fueled by contributions from the wealthy. Nonetheless, as our founding fathers and mothers understood, we cannot progress if we do not begin.

Democracy itself is imperiled in the U.S., and its survival is a central issue in this election. The forces of the incumbent president struck a powerfully destructive blow by hijacking the 2000 election and taking office against the expressed will of a plurality of the voters, and administration policies have continued this disenfranchisement. We who are American citizens need to be offered the opportunity to rebuild our faith in government. At the same time, we acknowledge that we need to be more responsible citizens and not just consumers of government. Democracy must be built and maintained. We view this election as an essential step in rebuilding our country.

This election will influence the shape of the world for years to come. For all its claims of being the party of realism, of patriotism, of standing up to our enemies, the Republican Party is actually the party of fear and self-interest, a party whose policies can lead only to the creation of Fortress America, assaulted on all sides. The Democratic Party offers the beginnings of a vision of a habitable world, a world whose members can realize their shared interests and potential and begin to work together. A vote for our party and our candidate is a vote for fair trade, fair business practices, constructive international collaboration, globally shared rules of behavior, equal rights and opportunities for all, and participation in a collective human effort to solve potentially catastrophic problems. With the validation of this election victory overwriting the shame of the stolen 2000 election, we will address the monumental challenges of reversing environmental degradation, preventing wars, and removing the threat posed by weapons of mass destruction.

We cannot accomplish this in four years. But with this vote, we can begin. We can make clear to the world the direction the United States will take. If the next administration is true to the principles we set forth here, other countries will follow. The difference in vision between this platform and the platform of our opponents is clear. We seek a united, cooperative humanity—a humanity that addresses the plight of its poor and dispossessed, a humanity seeking sustainable economies and technologies, a humanity that can bloom and flower in an environment of diminishing disparities in resource use and wealth and fewer wars and terrorist attacks.

If we fail, if the jingoistic voices of discord and fear triumph, the inevitable result, sooner or later, is an armed, environmentally degraded planet. It will be every nation, every corporation, every tribe, every interest group for itself.

George Bush and Dick Cheney ran in 2000 on a moderate, feel-good platform, then delivered unprecedentedly radical policies. Many voters did not know what they were voting for, that they were choosing abrogation of the Bill of Rights, a massive transfer of wealth to the already affluent at home, and empire abroad. Others were casting votes against Bill Clinton's embarrassing and undignified acts in the Oval Office.

If America elects the Bush-Cheney team, though, it will be a message to the world that we actually want them, that we endorse their swagger and lust for empire, that we no longer value our democracy, that we would rather dominate the planet and its resources by dog-eat-dog strategies than share the course of our destiny with the other peoples of the world. There will be no excuse this time, no avoiding the ultimate consequences of their perilous and self-serving tactics. Their arrogance will beget the arrogance of others, and our nation will suffer.

Poverty and injustice are the greatest weapons of mass destruction. They require no special technology, no strategic planning; they breed everywhere that we create their natural environments. They fester in darkness.

With this platform we seek to focus a bright, shining light on the United States in the 21st century. There is no question that enormous problems face our nation and the world. But the solutions are at hand. All we need do is seize the day.

And that day is November 2, 2004.

The Terra Nova Series

The Terra Nova Series comprises short texts by prominent twenty-first century authors exploring topics in the arts, cultural history, politics and international relations, and ethnic identity. The series is divided into **American Narratives,** statements from the American experience addressing a global context, and **Global Perspectives,** texts by international writers addressing the boundaries and interplay among nations, peoples, ideologies, and cultural representations.

Other books in The Terra Nova Series

American Narratives

Brando Rides Alone

A Reconsideration of the Film *One-Eyed Jacks*

Barry Gifford

$10.95 paper, 1-55643-485-5, 112 pp.

Seven Pillars of Jewish Denial

Shekinah, Wagner, and the Politics of the Small

Kim Chernin

$11.95 paper, 1-55643-486-3, 112 pp.

Global Perspectives

Empire 2.0

A Modest Proposal for a United States of the West by Xavier de C***

Prologue by Régis DeBray

$11.95 paper, 1-55643-495-2, 144 pp.

The Geneva Accord

And Other Strategies for Healing the Israeli-Palestinian Conflict

Rabbi Michael Lerner

$9.95 paper, 1-55643-537-1, 160 pp.
